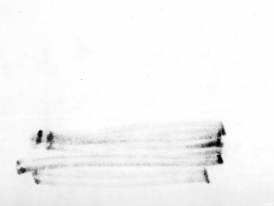

# ROAD TO REACTION

Professor Herman Finer was nurtured and educated in London, and studied at the University of London. He is the author of twenty-two books, including *The Theory and Practice of Modern Government*, *America's Destiny*, *The Major Governments of Modern Europe*, and *The Presidency: Crisis and Regeneration*. He is at present Professor of Political Science at The University of Chicago.

# ROAD

# TO

# REACTION

by HERMAN FINER

*With a New Introduction by the Author*

# E

ENCOUNTER PAPERBACKS

Quadrangle Books/Chicago

Till men have been some time free, they know not how to use their freedom . . . the final and permanent fruits of liberty are wisdom, moderation, and mercy. . . . If men are to wait for liberty till they become wise and good in slavery, they may indeed wait for ever.

— MACAULAY, ON MILTON

# Preface

> Out of such crooked material as man is made of,
> nothing can be hammered quite straight.
>
> — IMMANUEL KANT

Friedrich A. Hayek's *The Road to Serfdom* [1] constitutes the most sinister offensive against democracy to emerge from a democratic country for many decades. In writing this answer, I am not interested in winning an argument. That is far too easy. My grave anxiety is to keep the way open for democracy to make its own free, creative choices of public policy in the future. To build conservative barricades, altogether unamenable to change, as Hayek proposes, is to foment a violent explosion. Hayek and his courtiers have mistaken the nature and the temper of the times; and they trifle, or they would have come better equipped and without a peevish and rancorous temper. It is time to remind them of their responsibility before the freedom to do so is lost.

All men who love their country, especially after the sacrificial travail and the bereavements of the last few years, see that the true alternative to dictatorship is not economic individualism and competition, but democracy — that is, government fully responsible to the people. Such men experience a sinking of the heart that the distrust of and distaste for the

---

[1] The quotations from *The Road to Serfdom* throughout this book are used by kind permission of the University of Chicago Press.

v

common man exhibited in *The Road to Serfdom* could have received so warm an embrace.

His doctrine is this: As a way of planning production and distribution, competition is perfect in theory and practically so in action. Competition allows freedom to plan one's life without outside "arbitrary" interference. Private property is the guarantee of liberty, even for those who possess none, because it stops a government from having too much power. The power of government is corrupting even in democratic government, but economic power in the hands of individuals is not corrupting. "Planning" is "socialism"; socialism is "collectivism"; collectivism is "fascism," "nazism," and "communism" — or, in other words, planning is a dictatorship like those that have flourished in Europe. Hence, all the faults of dictatorship are the faults of planning by the state. Therefore, the state must enforce competition. And the way to safeguard this is to establish a bill of rights in the Constitution, enshrining the rights of competition; and the Constitution in that respect shall be altogether unamendable, the yoke fastened on the neck of democracy forever. Why such a drastic curtailment of the right of free and responsible decision? Because the majority cannot be trusted, for it may be "arbitrary." If there is government planning there is no Rule of Law, so the people must be curbed. There is to be as little planning for social security as possible. Democracy is a fetish and a fashion. Full employment is not the first priority in our future.

Reaction has been waiting yearningly for this message, for someone to smite democracy hip and thigh. It eases the conscience; approves the feeling that nothing need be done; attacks bureaucracy; says the planner is a scoundrel; and saves taxes! It is no surprise to students of politics, though it is to Hayek, that such a doctrine has been so widely acclaimed.

There is a responsibility on those who care for the well-being of the Republic to deal harshly with these contentions and the method used to support and commend them. For the most desperate task of the twentieth century, in our vast, teeming, complex societies, with structure towering upon structure, is to strengthen responsible government. Democracy that is responsible government, with all its present imperfections, is our salvation when we compare it with its cruel dictatorial rivals and with the forms of government under which mankind has groaned in the past. It is not property that gives liberty. That is Hayek's outstanding error. Liberty is the fruit of democracy. The people will not be shoved off the scene.

I have not had space here to discuss every one of Hayek's fallacies, for they are so many; they spring from every sentence, like the water from the leaks of a jerry-built ship. To put his sardonic prejudice and distorted contentions right would require an enormous volume. But what I have tried to show clearly is a way through the jungle of fallacies which have aspired to the dignity of an argument on a grand theme.

To do this the following chapters will show that Hayek's apparatus of learning is deficient, his reading incomplete; that his understanding of the economic process is bigoted, his account of history false; that his political science is almost nonexistent, his terminology misleading, his comprehension of British and American political procedure and mentality gravely defective; and that his attitude to average men and women is truculently authoritarian.

Whereas Hayek and his courtiers want for democracy the Closed Way, my persuasion is that justice and power rightly inhere in the people, who will have the Open Way to the future. They will not tolerate mortmain.

# Contents

# Contents

# INTRODUCTION

# The Road to Reaction Transformed

Since this work was first published and then went out of print, I have been deluged with requests for permission to use parts of it in anthologies, text-books, and reproductions for class and group use. I am glad that it can now be re-published in its complete version. Its subject matter is perennial: the problems involved in the public welfare, progress, and national security in a nation that has determined to stay free.

\* \* \*

Since World War II, the nations of the West, and many others, have succeeded in making spectacular advances in economic productivity and social welfare. Political leadership and business and labor, science and technology, the spirit of the masses, and those to whom they have looked for light and leading, have together achieved remarkable material progress not only without the loss of freedom, but with an increase of it, and with the growth of a sense that human relations are on a juster basis than they were. There is a general contentment that this is so.

Even as matters stood in the immediate aftermath of World War II, when the *Road to Reaction* was written, so now, but in a stronger sense, the greatest single factor of life in any modern society is Government. Men and women are affected daily by their churches, their cultural activities, art, the advance of science, sports, charity, the press and radio and television, but the more immense, the more embracing, the more suggestive and guiding power is that special instrument of liberty, order, and advance, Government. And it is neither an accident nor an evil conspiracy by politicians or public officials to grasp power. Power implies hard work, and neither of the two groups mentioned shows more appetite for more work and worry than their fellow citizens. The scope and depth of governmental functions issue with clear logic from the demands made by citizens for certain benefits and freedoms they need, which cannot be obtained by the spontaneous action of citizens organized by any lesser association than the nation. Every demand for a right by any person or group is, directly or indirectly, a demand for government. And the hundreds of thousands of demands add up. Nor are the demands arbitrary—for example, for protection from dangerous drugs. Friedrich A. Hayek, whose book, *The Road to Serfdom*,[1] called forth the answer in this book, made certain dire predictions that the trend to economic planning and social welfare in the hands of the government (that is, the political instrument of the national community) would produce dictatorship, and even a dictatorship of the lowest "criminal" elements of the nation. The fears, in a tone of threat, have simply not materialized. I predicted they would not, with reasons for my prognosis. The hopes entertained in my own work, that men equipped with modern minds, with social science, with a comprehension of their heritage, and with confidence in themselves, have been fulfilled, and will go on to more perfect fulfillment.

As I forecast: the United States and the lands of mainly free enterprises are *not* anywhere near totally planned. If anything, they enjoy a freer play of political and economic activity than ever before. Their processes of election and political leadership have the characteristics of what I then called the Open Way, and now are even more vigorous and independent in judgment than then. The free press flourishes even at times to anarchy and the margins of untruth, so hard does it hit society, individuals, and governmental leaders. Simultaneously, immense strides have been made in the increase of wealth, its juster distribution, the spread of opportunity, care for the unfortunate, and in the genius of scientific discovery and its application to human use.

The "conservatives" have been proved mean in spirit, erroneous in reasoning, and over-pessimistic about man's capacity for self-government and mastery of the nature of the social and physical world. The world has passed them by. For, in spite of their misanthropy and errors of observation, this is what the great modern democratic communities did, during the last twenty years. They brought in government gradually, only as the need for it was proved. They expanded the responsibility of government only remedially, as the failure of voluntary and local effort was demonstrated, in time, beyond a doubt. Their planning was not total, but only partial, applied to the segments of human activity proved beyond a doubt to need it, indeed, at their own outcry. The freedoms were maintained and even reinforced by political leadership and the action of the courts. The great corps of public officials, in nation, state, and city, were controlled in their behavior so that they should not degenerate into bureaucracy. The Open Way, or as it has come to be called, the Open Society,[2] was firmly maintained.

A review of the developed and developing relationship between government, business, and a free society must be given systematic consideration. Thus:

1. The Benefits and Necessity of Government
2. The Costs of Government
3. The Problems of Maintaining Freedom

## 1. *The Benefits and Necessity of Government*

Let the reader, in whatever station of life, profession, or occupation, try to imagine what life would be like, in the city or farm, without the services rendered to him and his family by government. That has actually become unthinkable, because those services are taken for granted just as much as the leg, the arm, the eyes, the brains of the individual. The recognition of what government performs for us, at our behest, may be put in this summary fashion: our home is no longer our castle because our home has expanded into our city, our country, our state, and our nation. The per capita wealth of American citizens, the highest in the world by far, is not the mere product of the isolated factory, or firm, or farm; that per capita of $2,500 per annum for man, woman, and child is in large part the product of the government's auxiliary, remedial, salvaging, corrective, guiding, co-ordinating, knowledge-finding and providing, for the economy by the government.[3] From the standpoint of all workers and employers, government is one more instrument of their economic need and expectations of a high standard of living.[4]

The detail is spelled out in the pages of this book. Any examination of the public budgets will tell the story: it is extremely difficult to find any items which can be reduced. This is because (a) the functions have been assumed by the taxpayer only after necessity is proven, sometimes postponed until the very last desperate moment (e.g., federal aid to education and to medical care); (b) each item ,though looked on critically by some group in the community, is, in a sense, the payment for some other item that the critic himself wants; and (c) all the items of public expenditure have, in the course of time, been fitted into a reciprocal relationship of benefit, e.g., farm supports and the need of steady purchasing budgets for education and defense.

What are the main benefits that modern democratic government tries to secure in a free society for its citizens? They fall into several categories, which due to restriction of space can only be tersely listed. Governmental responsibilities have been successfully demanded:

1. To raise the total standard of living, or, as we say nowadays, the Gross National Product, and to improve that of the individual.

2. To reduce hours of work, fatigue, and danger to health and life in the economy.

3. To redress inequality of opportunity and fortune among citizens by countering hereditary class positions of power and wealth through mass educational avenues.

4. To open the career and the enjoyment of life to the proper combination of brains and character regardless of class, sex, creed, or color.

5. To forestall depressions, mass unemployment, and the waste of unused plant capacity, by governmental guidance of investment, banking, and fiscal policy.

6. To regulate public utilities that, for geographical or technical reasons, are inclined to monopolistic interests and power.

7. To counteract the constant tendency to monoply in business generally, and by restoring multiple units of business, to induce competition which is the justification of free enterprise and guarantee of a free market for both consumers and producers.

8. To conserve natural resources against abuse by the present generation, and to re-invest in fertility where the abuse has occurred.

9. To defend the individual and the community from violence, injury, fraud, and disturbance of the peace; to render justice between parties and between persons and governmental bodies.

10. To defend the national community in its way of life, its survival, and its vital interests, economic and non-economic, against the threats made by other nations; and, for this purpose, to support the economies and defenses of scores of other nations, in especially attempting to win friends or avert the enmity, in case of clash, of many "new nations" in Africa and Asia, and old ones in Latin America, by economic aid of diverse kinds. All

activities under (10) require more than 60 per cent of the Federal national budget.

11. To promote a national-community sense of morality and justice: by family and divorce laws; limiting the licentious; suppressing fraud in business and the professions; sustaining the younger generation, the poor, the sick, the aged, by fostering mass education, libraries, artistic activities (the national and local community takes the place of the Medicis for modern Michelangelos who need patrons)—all this, by various measures, including social security, compassionate grant, or insurance arrangements.

If any spokesman of *laissez faire*, for example, a Senator Barry Goldwater,[5] announces that it is possible to reduce expenditure on any of these items or the number of career experts in public employ needed to do the job efficiently and expeditiously, let him answer precisely, with figures, how he intends to do it, and let him be asked to justify the community's losses in welfare and productivity that would follow.

The mere statement of the benefits of government is a statement of the necessity we all experience that government be vested with these powers and responsibilities. Yet something more may be added to give further foundation to the necessity: (a) the nature of the modern economy; (b) problems of equity and opportunity; (c) justice; (d) social morality; and (e) national survival.

(a) *The Modern Economy*.[6] The vital characteristics of modern economic enterprise in democratic communities are the acceptance of private property and the conduct of enterprise by the free entrepreneur. But what is the *spirit* of this kind of enterprise? It is a moral choice in which we all participate and connive: the attainment of the highest possible standard of living. This is almost the universal contemporary God, our highest practical creed.[7] The choice between wealth and poverty (these are relative terms) is a question of ethics, not economics. "The world is too much with us; late and soon, getting

xvi

and spending, we lay waste our powers . . . ," cried Wordsworth. Granted that we are the captives of a system that is already running, we could still make a different choice in the life of the family, the churches, art, culture, and *business* (including labor, of course): more or less material gain? If the answer is Yes, More . . . then governmental consequences follow.

To achieve maximum production, or gain, modern communities have developed the division of labor and the high specialization of skills. It can be expressed in Adam Smith's words, in 1776: A man nowadays makes not the whole of a pin, but only the eightieth part of a pin. Thousands of occupations and sub-occupations in industry, agriculture, commerce, transport, communications, finance, insurance, etc., contain within them scores of specialisms of science and technology and human relations, called administration or management. If this division is beneficial (each being highly expert), an instrument is necessary to assure that their special products, the bits and pieces, get assembled and marketed at the time the entrepreneurs planned, at the prices they estimated, so that they can recover the costs incurred in rent, planning staff, credit, insurance, salaries, wages, etc.

Above all, they want the government to guarantee industrial peace in order to avoid all the physical and planning dislocations that come of strikes and lock-outs; they want stability in government so they can calculate the national and local budgets, and therefore, the proportion of their product that will go in taxes, and the amounts the government will allow for expenses, depreciation, amortization, renewal of plant, etc. They want stability of the currency, or perhaps a slight continuing inflationary trend, because that is like catnip to employers, investors, and workers. Democracy is by nature inflationary. Yet all wish to have stability. They want to be sure of the integrity of the offers of supply of goods to them, of quality and costs, and they look critically at other entrepreneurs, like those of the General Electric Company who, in 1961, were found guilty of wrongful contract arrangements.

Now, government is called in, it is begged to come in, as soon as some of the weaknesses of the free economy are detected by businessmen themselves. The main kinds of such weakness are: that most firms are too small to develop the research of science and technology without government assistance and partnership, and, possibly, all are ignorant at some point of the effect of their individual and properly egotistical decisions on the costs and markets of all other firms in the nation (for example, the alternating glut and scarcity of farm products in years past). Furthermore, the competitive spirit does not always remain strong enough to push firms to the highest effort of mind and will and energy to increase productivity and reduce costs. Businessmen featherbed just as labor does. This is bad for total productivity in the community as a whole.[8] In addition, there are some risks a private firm will not run or cannot support, even if it is in a big consortium; TVA symbolizes this; the need of such economic facilities for the benefit of *all* firms together (roads, bridges, research) is evident, and their utility immensely adds to the nation's productive capacity.

Furthermore, a large percentage of the nation's economy derives from foreign trade. Business dumps heavily into the lap of government the consequences of opportunities to invest abroad (e.g., Middle East oil), trade barriers by importing countries, the balance of payments, and the value of the dollar at home and abroad.[9] Employers and workers therefore, through Congress and the Executive, create a governmental function. They demand the benefits that might be obtained by voluntary association for the purpose among businessmen, or if power and authority and discipline were exerted by their own organization over each of them, and if they paid dues for the consequent expense. Since this is inconvenient and inefficient, they must plead that the government provide the organization, functions, and authority to develop their private profit and wages, and when totaled, the increase in national wealth.

All that businessmen, workers, farmers, and others need to do to reduce the activities of government is to forego the benefits they ask of it.

One more thing must be added. In the United States, 70 per cent and more of the population lives in metropolitan areas.[10] This produces special problems of housing, water supply, policing for personal security, roadways from home to office and plant, lighting, sewage, etc. It is a curious and unfortunate phenomenon that such great agglomerations of people, served on the whole so well by their city administrations, seem to expect such services for nothing. But the truth is that their home is incomplete if confined to their house or apartment: those dwelling places would soon be uninhabitable if the city services were cut off. One's home is one's castle only on the assumption that the home is integrated in a larger home: the city and the services it renders. There is a price to be paid, and those so-called "conservatives" who run political campaigns on the slogan of reducing taxes must know in their minds and hearts that beyond a small margin they cannot give good civic services and simultaneously reduce the price they cost.

To repeat: Government is the instrument for the exchange of one kind of benefit among persons and groups for others; the exchange of some freedoms for others. Government results from the demand for rights by persons and groups; they can be free of government as soon as they reduce their demand for rights and benefits. In the present state of science and technology, and given the tradition of a high standard of living, this cannot happen.

Now, I merely add the other non-economic causes of governmental responsibilities.

(b) *Problems of Equity and Opportunity*. As a nation endures it develops a community consciousness and a conscience, concern for its moral standards and the obligation each man owes to others, simply as an obligation which would be manifested at home, in the street, in a club, or in a church, a virtue exercised towards one's neighbors.[11]

(c) *Justice*. What is a city, except an agglomeration of villages, living in close connection, a neighborhood of neighborhoods? Moreover, the Western nations, and the United States in particular, are suffused with Judeo-Christianity or other humane religions in which the highest injunctions are charity and mercy towards our fellow men. Is this to count for nothing? Is it possible to imagine the modern economic machine without its humanization by the credal ethics of Judeo-Christianity?[12] There are constitutional principles that follow from this, *all men are created equal* being the fundamental one. Men and women ask for justice. When it is beyond their own personal power, or beyond that of their family, or firm, they ask for it through their political parties. Hereditary obstructions to the rise and flowering of personal talent by those who begin life in poor families still exist. The main arm of government works to remedy this by educational opportunity. In this, the central government is implored to support and add to local governmental effort. Self-knowledge and knowledge of the world, with its spiritual heritage and its heritage of the achievements of genius, all the riches of culture, the intellect, and of science, are the greatest single gifts a community can make available to its members for the due use and comfort of their own inner resources. This also assists economic proficiency.

(d) *Social Morality*. St. Augustine said: "A state without a principle of justice, is nothing but a band of robbers." He meant that men without moral principle in their public life are nothing but materialistic log-rollers, pork-barrel scavengers. He is right. There are people in modern communities who, because of congenital weakness of character, mind, will, physique, wit, or youth or age, cannot rise to an independent subsistence. Are they to be abandoned, as some communities in the past exposed their infants and aged to the elements to kill them off? There is always the chance, a good chance, that some person who seems a weakling may be the parent of a genius. The grandfather of Lord Rutherford, who mastered the secrets of the nucleus of the atom and so gave to the world of economics and defense a power for good as well as evil, was a humble Scotch wheelwright. Compassion even pays! Democracy would go rotten and corrupt if it lost its compassion, especially when its standard of living is so tremendously high compared with all preceding centuries of man's existence. This is no plea for the malingerer, the panhandler.

(e) *National Survival.* The necessity is self-evident. Adam Smith said that it should be the maxim of a government that "Defense comes before opulence." We have the obligation to exert our moral standards in the world as a whole if we believe in them at home. To say they reach only the water's edge is to deny them the validity of principle, and its denial is exactly what makes for softness of character and loss of the society itself to some ruder nation.

## 2. *The Costs of Government*

The citizen has a double budget, both of which parts are highly integrated with each other: expenditure inside the home, and expenditure for the home that embraces and serves the home, without which his life would be "nasty, brutish, and short." Today the total budget of all governmental units in the United States, federal, state, and local, is $125 billion. This compares with a gross national product in 1962 of some $550 billion. It is a large proportion, 25 per cent. Could the other 75 per cent possibly amount to what it does without the remedial and auxiliary functions of government? The answer is no. The proportion has come to be much the same in all modern western communities, perhaps rather more in

Scandinavia, Britain, France, and Germany than in the United States.

The amount paid to government for its management on the citizens behalf is, still, substantial. It can be lowered for some sections of the community, and it can be levied in forms that do not produce damage to growth and equity, by wise fiscal policy. It is possible that according to its form of being levied the tax burden may decrease enterprise. Ways of avoiding this are always in the process of study and legislation. But it must be understood that taxes represent good and even indispensable values.[13]

The funds are managed by public officials. The amount of actual illegal expenditures is almost infinitesimal. But it is not possible to dispense with some 2,500,000 public servants in the employ of the federal government, and some six million by the states and cities. What are they? They are all more or less capable experts in some special field of the administrative, social, natural, and physical sciences: an architect, a town planner, a farm-fertility scientist, an engineer who inspects the airports and the control of air safety (because the entrepreneur and sometimes the pilots take chances with human *life*, for gain or kicks); a sanitary inspector; a roadway builder and maintainer; a cancer researcher; a discoverer of space science, and so on and so on.

No one likes paying taxes; but who *likes* paying the dentist or the supermarket cashier? It needs more reason and enlightenment to realize that the totally indispensable services of government must be paid for also and that they are perhaps more basic, more urgent than the private service.

The cost of government today is double what it was in 1945, but in that period the gross national product has doubled also. The chief increase in government expenditure has come from the increase for national defense, and from that hundreds of thousands of families earn their living in the arms and research plants.

## 3. *The Problems of Maintaining Freedom*

Most human beings like enjoyment without employment. Most human beings like the services of government while they clamor for local government and self-government. This is the paradox of human nature: to want the fruits of centralization while keeping local and personal and state rights that militate against the benefits of large-scale organization.

Now, the anxieties about the increase in governmental activity, or what is called "the public sector," are these: (a) the loss of initiative available to private persons; (b) the loss of initiative and discretion available to local government; (c) the loss of control over the "bureaucracy," better expressed as public employees, no different in their desires and character than you or I; and (d) the peril from lobbyists or special groups.

(a) When government takes over a function previously managed by private enterprise, e.g., housing or medical care, the latitude for personal initiative is to that extent decreased. It is the same when investment is regulated because it is abused by swindling men and women: the freedom to swindle is restricted. The rule then should be to suit the reduction of initiative, or the amount and kind of governmental responsibility, strictly and appropriately to each case. This, in a government such as that of the United States with its separation of powers and checks and balances, occurs.

All government is the exchange of some freedoms for others. The question always has been and is whether the exchange of freedoms is, on balance, the most valuable that human reason can devise.

(b) Many of the activities of government—demanded by the outcry of citizens, e.g., the abatement of smoke in the cities, better educational provisions throughout the nation (with a kind of national minimum regardful of the inequality of wealth of our various states and cities), a modern highway system—necessarily centralize. This is because the most expert people are few and are employable by the central authority; because the principles are established in Washington; because inspection of quality of service is by federal or state officials. This seems to leave less room for local *self*-government to the localities and the professions.

Two things must be said about this criticism. First, an enormous field was always open to the localities if they wished to exercise their initiative. Neither the states nor the smaller municipal units have done so in as sufficient or as competent a manner as modern living requires. Which city can afford to build cyclotrons? Which can make a Telstar? Which can, of itself, build tollways and bridges and harbors? Which has even wanted to do so? Which has been able to provide a detective service as honest and unconniving and efficient as the F.B.I.? Any one of them could have spent all its budget on one of these items alone—but what of the rest of its needs: the process of association in the greater commonwealth, needed to assure the functions of civilized life?

Secondly, there still remains an immense amount of work to be done at the local level; the room for practical everyday co-operation in all the public services is vast. If it is desired that democracy shall be strengthened by participation in public service, then the field is wide; a counterweight to public officials and central executives and legislators is fully available. Indeed, if the powers of the center have increased, so have the powers of the states and the cities. Yet we must always hold to the principle: to decentralize wherever you can, centralize only where you must. For each addition to the central authority is a burden, and this, in itself, *might* introduce inefficiencies and inhumanities. Each case is a separate one that must be measured by itself. The acidulous and pretentious generalities of the Barry Goldwaters are most frequently spurious.

(c) This leads directly to the fundamental question: Can the public employees growing greatly in number be spurred on to do their best intellectually and with imagination and energy? Every government department, I have said, is in the nature of monopoly; it has the potential defects of monopoly whether in business or in any other sphere of life, that is, it may possibly *not* act according to the principle or law that sets it up to do a job for the benefit of its clients, or take notice of its coordination with collateral departments. Now, in business the regulator of efficiency is what may be called Consumer Sovereignty. Every firm must earn its dollars from the customer, who can vote against its prosperity and put it in the red simply by spending his money elsewhere. It is true that in private enterprise the tricks of advertising and monopoly and oligopoly (a clique of firms in collusion) can defeat the sovereign power of the consumer and his dollar. But by and large it works, especially if policed by the government and the law.

When a function is managed by a public department it is financed by taxes, and the customer cannot go elsewhere. The substitute for Consumer Sovereignty is Voter Sovereignty. But that can only do the job if the political parties acknowledge and honor the responsibility by setting up the pattern of a good society in their platforms; honoring them as commitments; and, almost, I would say, above all, organizing the committee supervision of the departments in Congress in a modern way designed to secure efficiency.[14] Yet Congressmen have often been connivers in dishonor and have exploited public officials for their own clients.[15] This is a central issue. I and others have raised this question in several works.[16] Congress needs reform from this point of view, urgently, drastically.[17] It is a miracle that the public service is now recruited and disciplined in such a way that the moral responsibility of the employees themselves keeps the machinery and processes of government so sane and clean and virile.[18]

(d) Finally, these considerations raise another. It is the one that appears in President Dwight D. Eisenhower's

Farewell Address; and surely, it is addressed more to businessmen and organized labor, as well as the citizenry in general, than to the public officials, I mean, in the sense of imputing responsibility for exploitation of the public welfare for the ends of private persons and pressure groups.

This is the main point that he makes: "This conjunction of an immense military establishment and a large arms industry," Eisenhower said, "is new in the American experience. . . . In the councils of Government, we must guard against the acquisition of unwarranted influence, whether sought or unsought, by the military-industrial complex. . . We must never let the weight of the combination endanger the liberties of democratic processes. . . ."

He did not spell it out, or analyze its consequences. It is in reality an appeal against private pressure groups in industry and among the military, where the budget is nearly $60 billion for defense alone. Those who maintain vested interests in this expenditure, and attempt to increase it even where certain products are not necessary, operate against the interests of local government and state powers, and make possible connivance among lobbyists, intermediaries, and influence-peddlers, and promote the undermining of the objectivity of public officials.

Still, when we think of all the progress our society has made since 1945, when *Road to Reaction* was first published to criticize the pessimistic and misanthropic fallacies of Hayek's *The Road to Serfdom*, and the work of lesser men, like Senator Barry Goldwater and his blinkered companions, we may count our blessings.

The United States is renowned because it is woven of the strands of the *Free Moral State;* the *Welfare State* (a term that came into use only about 1948); the *Economic Partner State;* and the *World Leadership State.* All that has happened since 1945 has enhanced the benefits of these qualities and held in check the deleterious elements that may be found mixed with all that is good in the individual, the locality, the group, or the world in general. Brains and character in a free society will sustain the continuance of this progress.

The bibliography (as footnotes) has been designed to bring the reader up to date about both the theory and practice of the themes of the *Road to Reaction.*

1. Cf., Friedrich A. Hayek, *The Constitution of Liberty* (Chicago, 1960). It is an expanded version of *The Road to Serfdom,* full of learning and adduced facts, but with no advance, I venture, in comprehension.

2. Cf., Herman Finer, *Major Governments of Modern Europe* (New York, 1962), for a depiction of the practical and theoretical lineaments of the free societies of Britain, France, Germany, and (allusively) the United States, compared with the dictatorial political and economic institutions of the Soviet Union. Also, Karl Popper, *The Open Society,* revised edition (London, 1957).

3. Cf., Merle Fainsod and others, *Government and the American Economy* (New York, 1959); and the Economic Report of the President to the U.S. Congress, January 1963.

4. John Kenneth Galbraith, *The Affluent Society* (Boston, 1958).

5. Barry Goldwater, *The Conscience of a Conservative* (New York, 1960), and *Why Not Victory?* (New York, 1962).

6. Paul Samuelson, *Economics* (New York, 1961); John Kenneth Galbraith, *American Capitalism* (Boston, 1956); Raymond W. Goldsmith, *The National Wealth of the United States in the Postwar Period* (Princeton, 1962).

7. R. H. Tawney, *The Acquisitive Society* (London, 1927 and subsequent editions); and United States Congress, 86th Congress, 1st Session, Doc. 46283, Joint Economic Committee, *Comparisons of United States and Soviet Economics,* Parts I, II, and III, and *Hearings* on same.

8. Cf., *Goals for Americans,* Report of the President's Commission on National Goals, by Henry M. Wriston and others (New York, 1961); Rockefeller Fund, *Prospect for America* (New York, 1961), especially Reports of Panel, IV, V, and

VI. (The other reports therein, on foreign policy, are also of great importance.) See, further, "Conservatism, Liberalism, and Nationalism," *Annals of the American Academy of Political and Social Science*, November 1962; Calvin B. Hoover, *The Economy, Liberty and the State* (New York, 1961); J. S. Dupré and S. A. Lakoff, *Science and the Nation* (Englewood Cliffs, 1962); Don K. Price, *Government and Science* (New York, 1962); Stephen K. Bailey, *et al*, *The Economics and Politics of Public Education* (Syracuse, 1962).

9. Robert Goldwin, ed., *Foreign Aid* (Chicago, 1963).

10. Lewis Mumford, *The City in History* (New York, 1961), and *Transformations of Man* (New York, 1956); The Editors of Fortune, *The Exploding Metropolis* (New York, 1958); Werner Z. Hirsch, ed., *Urban Life and Form* (New York, 1963); F. Stuart Chapin and Shirley F. Weiss, *Urban Growth Dynamics* (New York, 1962).

11. Cf., Bishop William Scarlett, ed., *The Christian Demand for Social Justice* (New York, 1949); Robert T. Harris, *Social Ethics* (Philadelphia, 1962).

12. A. S. Miller, ed., *The Ethics of Business Enterprise* (Philadelphia, 1962).

13. A. E. Holmans, *United States Fiscal Policy, 1945-1959* (New York, 1961); Message of the President on Tax Reform, January 23, 1963.

14. James MacGregor Burns, *The Deadlock of Democracy* (Englewood Cliffs, 1963).

15. Bernard Schwartz, *The Professor and the Commissions* (New York, 1959); Charles S. Hyneman, *Bureaucracy in a Democracy* (New York, 1950); Peter Woll, *American Bureaucracy* (New York, 1963).

16. Cf., Herman Finer, *The Presidency: Crisis and Regeneration* (Chicago, 1960).

17. George Galloway, *The Legislative Process in Congress* (New York, 1953).

18. Bertram M. Gross, *The Legislative Struggle* (New York, 1953); David Truman, *Congressional Party* (New York, 1959); J. W. Fulbright, *et al*, *The Elite and the Electorate* (Fund for the Republic, Santa Barbara, California, 1963).

# ROAD TO REACTION

CHAPTER I

# The Day before Yesterday, and Tomorrow

"They may remember yesterday, but they forget the day before." This was the comment made by Professor E. W. Kemmerer when he was asked by the Senate in 1931 whether the crass mistakes made by business which had brought on the great depression would be remembered by the people. The question was important, for, if a democracy forgets, democracy will be forgotten, and may be crushed by the economic forces it ignores.

It is certain that even over the intervening tragedy of World War II, that calamitous failure of the competitive order will long continue to be remembered. The most important historic consequence of the great depression was its grim, detailed, and unchallengeable demonstration of the chronic deficiencies of unbridled competition as the governor of the modern economic system. The sharpest lesson of all was the general loss of confidence in that order's ability to do the work expected of it. Every group participating in it at some time and for some special reason expressed distrust in it, and a sense of insecurity in living within it.

The failure of private enterprise in the depression was not a small and casual aberration. Savings and homes and farms were swept away. Life insurance had to be liquidated to meet current budgets and debts. Educational funds (if not lost in the banks where they had been fondly deposited) were drawn and spent. Many suffered starvation; more,

3

malnutrition. Necessary medical attention had to be post-poned. Social expenditures by city and township were abruptly stopped until public works were instituted to prime the pump. Enveloping all, like a dreadful and menacing miasma, were fear, insecurity, and humiliation. The fault, as was demonstrated by every private and public inquiry, was hardly ever a fault of individual character among the victims, it was a fault of the system: men and women begged for work, private enterprise could not give it. The National Industrial Conference Board estimated that at the depression's severest point 11,864,000 were unemployed; that was in 1933. In 1930, the figure was nearly 3,000,000; thenceforward to 1941 it was never below 6,413,-000. There are other estimates which give much higher figures.

Corresponding to the extent of unemployment was the loss of production. It has been estimated that if there had been only two million unemployed each year during 1929–1937, the United States would have produced in those nine years goods worth two hundred billion dollars (at 1929 prices) more than were actually produced. This is two and a half times the total national production of the United States in 1929. It is also four times as much as the total income of Great Britain, Canada, Australia, South Africa, New Zealand, and Germany in 1929. A comparison of the depression year (1932 or 1933, according to the country concerned) with 1929 disclosed for the United States a loss of 51 per cent of its national income; for Germany, 41 per cent; for France, 19 per cent; for Great Britain, 12 per cent. Elsewhere, declines of 20 and 30 per cent were common. At the depth, in 1932, over twenty-five million industrial workers were unemployed throughout the world — which may represent the destitution of a hundred million people, when the families are included.

Appalling as the catastrophe was, it was not a single and

nonrecurrent event. Depression is a chronic disease of the competitive system. Twenty times, between 1854 and 1933, had the United States suffered such disasters, of varying severity; other countries had been equally afflicted.[1] It can happen twenty times again.

The sense of desperation produced by the downward tug of economic ruin subjected political systems throughout the world to tremendous strain. In Germany, still a democratic form of government, people (especially those in command of the economic order) flew for help to men who were making ready to supplant popular government by dictatorship. In France, the nation was split wide open socially. In the United States and Great Britain, where the democratic system had firmer foundations in the history and character of the people, the gravest pressure, almost to the breaking point, was put on the constitutions, which barely survived.

Two effects of the inter-war depression soon became indelibly manifest: all participants in economic production rushed to their government clamoring for rescue; and public and private investigation into the causes revealed the inevitability of distress under the untrustworthiness of enterprise conducted within the competitive system. In the United States it was demonstrated — literally in scores of thousands of pages of testimony and cross-examination in Congressional Committees before interrogators not anxious to convict the culpable but only to find an explanation and a way out — that those engaged in the productive process, particularly those who directed the great corporations, practised their calling in such a way as to make the competitive system antisocial in its effects. The extremely detailed examination showed that financiers, bankers, and stockbrokers had restricted competition, obstructed free price movements, made foreign loans without even a considera-

[1] *Cf.* Burns and Mitchell, Table 139, in *Measuring Business Cycles* (N. Y., 1945).

tion of responsibility to home manufactures, bribed foreign politicians to take loans from them for useless public works, erroneously predicted their own markets, and falsified essential information to the purchasing and investing public.

It was shown that industrialists had restricted the output of goods below the capacity of their equipment and plant and technical skill, in order to hold up prices; that they had stimulated purchasing on credit beyond rational consideration of future employment and earning hazards, suppressed inventions by antisocial manipulation of patent restrictions, and expanded and contracted credit for self-regarding profit purposes alone. Holding companies, after contriving strategic financial control over pyramids of public utility corporations, especially the electric power industry, had extracted payments from them on pretended but not actual services rendered to the several corporations, and so had levied high charges on the public, permitted to do so by public utility control commissions who were misled by the chicanery of the directors cited to answer charges before them. Politicians were let in on profitable investments as compensation for unstated services. The credit and banking systems of the several states were almost everywhere without sound foundations of law and practice, and without guarantee of either character or correct procedure; speculation, even gambling, on investment and industrial hazards was rife; insurance companies were without due inspection for standards of sober business conduct by the states which chartered them. Enormous private and municipal indebtedness had been piled up under the high-pressure, unscrupulous operations of salesmen and moneylenders.

Finance, industry and agriculture, at profit-seeking odds with each other, had acted without vision, measure, or sense of a comprehensive good-for-all society, preventing the rise of a stable and integrated relationship between them. There was no social provision in case of disaster: practically no public employment exchanges (Mr. Hoover indignantly refused to set them up even when the disaster had arrived), no unemployment insurance, no public works or development schemes, no public medical schemes, no substantial poor-relief system. People were trusting to the claims that the unregulated, unassisted competitive system could give prosperity, and even fortunes; when disaster retorted with the lie demonstrative, it was disaster, indeed.

Worst of all in the desperate situation which ensued was the negative response of big industry and finance — the grand beneficiaries of competition (such as they had made it) in good times. They had no plan for improvement to propose to the committees of investigation other than to leave things alone and let matters take their course in the usual hands, their own. There might perhaps be a more deliberate restriction of competition as compared with the informal and unsanctioned monopolistic practices already prevalent — in the form of the self-government of the various industries, if the government cared to help in its establishment. But above all, things must take their course. The advice to Congress by the leading machinators of the order of competition was perfectly summed up by Mr. Hoover in the White House in the conviction that "prosperity is just round the corner," and in reliance upon God. "Under the guidance of Divine Providence," he declared on June 15, 1931, "they ["the intellectual and spiritual forces leading to success unparalleled in world history"] will return to us a greater and more wholesome prosperity than we have ever known." The principal plan of the Chambers of Commerce for stemming the flood of the depression was to set up codes of business conduct, to be administered by each industry. They fondly recommended that the antitrust laws be so modified as to permit industry to limit competition, to raise prices and to restrict production!

The most handsome monument to this planlessness was

the Reconstruction Finance Corporation, the government's life line to business. In 1931, it represented "capitalism on the dole," though since then that institution has become a very promising and indispensable instrument of government assistance to developing enterprise. As *Fortune*[2] said of October 4, 1931, when President Hoover met the great bankers at Mr. Andrew Mellon's house, "Bitter must have been Mr. Hoover's task that day. All around him lay the ruins of his dreams of prosperous times. . . . Something had to be done — at once." The start, with half a billion dollars to bail out the railroads, banks, insurance and mortgage loan companies, and various other financial institutions, was a tragicomical commentary on the President's answer to those who were now begging for bread: "Not regimented mechanisms, but free men is our goal." As for business, not this one depression, but the secular experience of the United States, showed that "rugged individualism" had become drugged individualism. It is of the utmost importance to realize that all the basic remedial measures of these times — R.F.C., the Banking Act, Farm Credit, social security, control of public utilities, farm security, T.V.A., improvement of the Federal Reserve system, the Securities and Exchange Commission, the Fair Labor Standards Act, a reactivated antitrust policy, the great boards and commissions of inquiry into the social deficiencies of the American Republic and the structure and operation and future of American industry, the Housing Act, the Farm Tenant Act — are the indispensable props of private enterprise. There would be a gasp of horror at the resultant insecurity and inefficiency if these were taken away.

Naturally, the investigations dissipated confidence in the authority and prestige of the unwearied titans of the economic system. What these men did in the market was

[2] May 1940.

8

regarded as smart and even illustrious; but its results were so painful to millions upon millions that the churches, civic groups, universities, and the spokesmen and conscience of American society were compelled to declare that something must be done, or else the directly and indirectly distressed might turn to the Russian experiment for guidance!

One Senate Committee revealed that shipbuilding and associated firms had employed a lobbyist to do his best to frustrate international naval limitation at Geneva in 1930, for the sake of additional orders. The suicide of Ivar Kreuger in Paris was another sensational scandal of the time. The Senate brought to light that this super-Napoleonic organizer of no less than 140 match companies in half a dozen countries had had the continuous support of famous American banking and brokerage houses. Three hundred names notable in the highest of all American banking and brokerage circles had helped to sell some quarter of a billion dollars' worth of debentures, the return for which was to come from the revenues of the match monopolies of many foreign governments. Kreuger and Toll — the firm which manipulated this great international exchange of values — had spoofed their American co-operators with false information about their capital, the value of the foreign concessions, the amount of the revenues to be expected, the collateral they held as guarantee, and had had the accounts certified by accountancy firms of their own appointing. In this investigation also it was revealed that some promoting bankers evaded the federal income tax by deducting losses on bonds; they sold the bonds (as the law required, for deduction) at a low price, to friends — and then took them back again later.

Samuel Insull, Chicago manipulator of public utility holding companies capitalized at about two billion dollars in a network spread over the United States from Maine to Oklahoma and Texas, and said to be personally worth some one hundred and seventy million dollars, had to be chased

9

all the way to Greece, to be extradited for fraud. He had deceived the public in his watering of stocks, overcharging for services to the companies, marking up the values of their assets, urging the purchase of bonds which, on a moment's responsible reflection, he must have known were worthless. He had deceived the political custodians of the public interest, or seduced them from their responsibility by money bribes.

The Senate made clear to the world many years of shady financial practices and a system of "graft" within big business easily superior, in subtlety of swindling, to that practised by the most sophisticated political boss. Great firms like the House of Morgan were compelled to make the choice between continuing as bankers or as investment houses: the tie-up between the two professions had not been good for the public, and tore the conscience of the operators into too many pieces to insure a prudent responsibility towards their clients.

In the spring of 1938, Richard Whitney was convicted of grand larceny for misappropriation of customers' securities, in the amount of about 435,000 dollars; and his firm, with nearly four million dollars of liabilities and few assets, was declared insolvent. "Ironically enough, in the light of his misappropriations of customers' securities which have been traced back to 1926," says the report of the Securities and Exchange Commission, he was "the Chairman of the Committee on Business Conduct from 1928 to 1929, and a member of that Committee for many years prior to 1928." This was a committee of the New York Stock Exchange; Richard Whitney had been President of the Exchange itself from 1930 to 1935. He had held many other important positions on the governing bodies of the Exchange for many years past. In the course of the Commission's proceedings against him he was shown to have made great personal extravagant expenditures; to have been borrowing for many years from friends and firms without disclosure of his firm's financial condition; to have misrepresented this from time to time when suspicion was aroused or when otherwise convenient; to have undertaken financial speculations outside the usual course of his own business, of an unsound and ruinous nature. It was shown that various persons on the Exchange had reason to have suspicions of his insolvency long before this was unearthed in 1938, but had not exercised that rigorous degree of inquiry required for the proper discovery of incompetence and dishonesty. It was shown also that the House of Morgan had assisted Richard Whitney with loans without severe enough inquiry into their purpose or economic justification, without the full disclosure of appropriate information from one partner to another, and without adequate interrogation by one partner of another; a brother of Whitney was a partner in the House of Morgan.

Behind all these revelations was the sharp contour of the seven-decade-long story of monopolistic practices: the theoretical benefits of competition were not fulfilled, neither was security obtained.

In Great Britain, where government is more pervasive of society and economy, where social life is more integrated, and where social security schemes date back to 1911, with very enhanced provisions since the end of World War I, scandals of the dimensions unearthed in the United States were not features of competitive industry, though there were some involving shipping, the purchase of municipal bonds, the attempt to corner some commodity markets. But, as in the United States, there was a decline and lack of inclination for competition on the part of business, and the scourge of unemployment, neither of which could be cured except by governmental assistance. Government was, with two short and unimportant intervals, in the hands of the Conservative Party. There was much attention to the reorganization of British trade to meet foreign competition, and the government assisted this movement, sometimes even required it, as the inertia of the industries themselves threatened to leave British economy further behind than ever in the race for technical efficiency. Various marketing schemes and the modernization of production methods were supported by government subsidies. The industries themselves, and various governmental investigating committees, admitted that the day of sheer competition was over; they reported the necessity for trade organizations and proceeded to the establishment of such organizations with government help. At the same time, there was a steady development of the adverse side of monopoly, namely price control and output restriction. This is still an unsolved problem.

One of the solutions sought in the United States, the provision of public work, was only to a very small extent feasible in Great Britain as the Conservative Party detested such a solution. Their policy was that of the minimum public assistance compatible with the public conscience and public order, with special care against high taxes. The policy therefore was unemployment insurance, and when the term of such payments ran out, "the dole." But this did not abolish or reduce unemployment, though it piled up expenditures; nor did it give men back their self-respect. It did not rehabilitate the large areas of the country which had come to be called "derelict" or "special areas," where towns had been "murdered" by the flight of industry from them. Since the total cost of relief had to be kept down, severe tests of the means of the applicant were made; and, since some of the burden was by law to fall on the members of the family who were still in work, the unemployed were made to feel that they were a burden on those in work, while the younger members of the family were restricted in their freedom to move away or marry because they had to meet their share of the household budget. There were unemployed marches and hunger marches, and riots against the scale of relief payments. There were the most shocking distress and undernourishment. Finally, when the Labour government of 1929-1931 insisted on maintaining the scale of payments in spite of a small but growing budget deficiency, a coalition of Conservative and Liberal leaders forced upon them the choice between cutting down the payments and reducing the deficiency and taxation, and leaving office. They left office, with the exception of Ramsay MacDonald and a few followers, who joined with the Conservative Party and the Liberal Party to form a government which solved the problem by making the cuts and at the same time acquiring extra revenue by the imposition of tariffs, and by giving a fillip to trade by abandoning the gold standard. The fall of the Labour government was not unassisted by whispers that American bankers had refused loans to Britain unless that should take place.

In the United States and Great Britain, the failure of the free competitive system to produce an industrial order that could stably and steadily produce a proper plenty for all caused critical pressures upon the democratic system and the constitutional conventions upon which that is founded. The governments were not sensitively responsive to the distress and the panic. For a long time they pretended they saw no evil, heard no evil, but that to act was evil. The Hoovers and the Landons tried strong resistance. The mind of the Supreme Court underwent the ordeal of conversion, lest worse befall.

The depression crisis and its pressure on the constitutional democracy of both the United States and Great Britain would have become unpredictably grave if World War II had not supervened. Serious social psychoses would have beaten frantically against democratic forms. In Great Britain, every constitutional form and convention was strained to the utmost. The feelings and conscience of the public were aroused and confidence subverted by the actions and breakdown of the very economic institutions, and their coadjutors and abettors in government, that required, above all, public calm and confidence in them for steady operation. To offset this perturbation, the defenders of the system of free and competitive enterprise sought for dependable weapons. In the long run, the most dependable political weapon is persuasion; and, in a democracy, it is almost fatal to try anything else. The persuasion they sought must be such as morally to absolve their own consciences, by explaining the value of their own economic function and justifying the inevitability of their own exclusive fulfillment of it, whether happy or unhappy. The system and the men were indispensable. It was necessary to show that what had happened in the depression (and what might happen again) was not their personal fault, but part of a system, of which they themselves were only small parts; that those who were its chief executives themselves took losses as well as gains, and were, in short, merely agents; and that the order they represented and served was really beneficent, even if its myriad victims were too stunned with distress at once to comprehend and accept it.

To accomplish this task of persuasion there was no lack of champions.

# CHAPTER II

# The Reactionary Manifesto

No passion so effectually robs the mind of all its
powers of acting and reasoning as fear.
— EDMUND BURKE

If the champions of an economic and political delu-
sion were its only victims, we could with a little charity
leave them to their rude awakening. But in democratic
countries delusions may become public policies, supported
by power, and hungry for domination even at the cost of
subverting democracy.

It is obvious that to some thousands of people the fact
that Friedrich A. Hayek's *The Road to Serfdom* is the
Manifesto of the reactionaries does not disqualify it as a
contribution to proper public policy. Those who, like Hayek,
sum up "Let us go back in order to jump higher" can, in
our political situation, be nothing but the worshipers of
reaction. His book is the arsenal of the conservative counter-
offensive. It is full of the weapons designed to destroy and
scatter mankind's generous but hardheaded self-confidence
that acute economic and social problems can be solved by
democracy. Here is a joy for all conservatives. In spite of
the world's desperate travail to overthrow Hitler and Mussolini and what they have stood for, many conservatives need
the new joy because secretly they have just lost the old one.

We now live in a world without Hitler. His removal has
swept away the inhibition against open avowal of his doctrines of contempt for the majority and equality and popular

sovereignty. There will be a babel of antidemocratic statements within a few months; murmuring can already be
heard. For a time the bitterness of the reactionaries has been
merely bridled, out of expediency, while the power and
repute of the majority have been magnified, because it is the
majority that fights world wars.

America and Britain have now fully returned to the tasks,
and the antagonists in each to the political feelings and
methods, of the inter-war years. Briefly, the issue is whether
or not the kind of social and economic progress made,
especially since 1933 in the United States and since 1906 in
Great Britain — that is, the remedying of the shocking
deficiencies of private, economic enterprise, and the positive
contribution of the state to the raising of the standard of
living by its economic initiative — shall continue and be
increased. The issue is not settled. Let no one believe that
those who were overruled in open, democratic, and peaceful
electoral contest accept the fact. The kind of spirit of governmental enterprise represented by the parties in power in the
years mentioned above is alien to them. What is true, tragi-
comically true, is the fact that the conservative reactionaries
have, in Hayek, hugged a viper to their breasts. It is far
better policy for them to listen to critics than to flatterers.

The reasons for the welcome to the Manifesto are plain,
but should have been the objects of instantaneous suspicion.
The Manifesto is stuffed with banners, bans, and a bogeyman. Its banners are magnificent: freedom, liberty, liberalism, individualism, the Rule of Law, morality, enterprise,
and property. They are the standards of us all. Its bans are
obvious: Nazi-Socialism, fascism, and communism. They
are the bans of us all. Its bogeyman is planning, which is
identified as dictatorship. Planning, as a fate that cannot be
controlled or fled, must call down the bans on the heads of
all and destroy the banners. Murderers and hangmen
must get to the top in a society of planning, says Hayek.

16

The palatability of this sour prejudice owes most to its argument that the successful businessman, and all those aspiring to be successful, are rendering a greater economic service to the public than planners could ever do; that, indeed, by acting as private enterprisers they hold the banners high.

For this, the conservatives were athirst: a creed to justify private enterprise, which had shown itself capable of a great depression, many permanent and grave faults of organization, and, as the Pecora investigation revealed, violation of common morality. The restoration of their moral standing, shaken badly by public clamor they would rather evade and by their own uncovered misdemeanors, is their persistent quest. Not that they have lost an interest in lots of money, but they like honor as well.

We can understand those who have made Hayek's book the companion of their bosoms, bought great quantities and distributed them among those waiting with watering mouths for its advent, or reproduced it in popular digests and scattered it broadcast. Like ourselves, they are parts of humanity, with difficult problems of existence, philosophical and economic, and not quite so clever and powerful as most people would like to be. But they have got hold of the wrong champion because he tried to be too strong a champion.

To be easy in their republic, they must have an easiness about the republic inside themselves. They are *not,* as Hayek crudely pretends that they are, men whose economic outlook is severable from their outlook as men. Only apparitions are dissectible in economic seminars; men are whole and alive. "Man is by his constitution," said Edmund Burke, "a religious animal."

There is not one sphere of private business, and another of government. There never has been. But our times are such that their relationship forces fundamental questions upon the businessman as well as upon society. This relationship has been the cockpit of politics in Western Europe, Britain, and the United States during the inter-war years, for three reasons: the disturbance of traditional morality by World War I; the forcing of state-planned production and distribution during that war; and the rise of an entirely novel economy: Soviet Russia. It is the last that men have not been able to cast out of their consciousness. For somewhere, in the real world that they know, there exists a titanic working model of all that they were reared to abhor! This has produced the most bewildering perplexities — far more in the United States than in Great Britain, where more people feel more easily confident about their ability to control their government. Some men who should have known better — Max Eastman, W. H. Chamberlin, and Eugene Lyons to mention a few — threw all their bread upon the waters of Russian Communism, and, of course, it came back moldy. These, too, more articulate than the businessman, look for a creed. They are warm welcomers of the Manifesto, and again they are doomed to have their bread come back moldy.

Breaking the taboo on discussion, Hayek is almost the first to reject the principle of full employment. (Page 206.) In doing this, he has scant regard for the fact that over and above the aims of World War I, those of World War II concern economic prosperity and social justice. I do not mean that either Great Britain or the United States entered the war to destroy the inequities and inefficiencies in their own economic and political systems. Neither entered the war until the issue of its national survival had been sharply raised against it, though there were some valorous millions who could not tolerate a moral vacuum in themselves or moral isolation for their country. The democratic nations found themselves fighting governments whose ideals were not only murderously hostile to theirs, but were openly declared so to be. Hitler declared that dictatorship and democracy could not live in the world together. This implied a rejection of the principles of the democratic system. Were those who fought against Hitler fighting *for* these democratic principles? Only the future can tell, and can show with what understanding, consciousness, and emotional loyalty. This however is certain, that the governments and the press told their soldiers that they were fighting for certain bases of public policy and that in future practice these would be broadened. As important as any of the principles which were pronounced were jobs and social security; these were the minimal equities for the defense of the social framework. In the United States this took the form of the announcement of the Four Freedoms, which it is not amiss to repeat: —

"In the future days, which we seek to make secure, we look forward to a world founded upon four essential human freedoms." They were: freedom of speech; freedom of worship; freedom from fear; and freedom from want — "which, translated into world terms, means economic understandings which will secure to every nation a healthy peacetime life for its inhabitants."

Later in that year the Atlantic Charter contained the aspiration that the nations would proceed to secure "for all improved labor standards, economic advancement, and social security." And on January 11, 1944, came the Presidential announcement of a "second bill of rights," and the theme that "true individual freedom cannot exist without economic security and independence." These rights were: the right to a useful and remunerative job; the right to earn enough to provide adequate food and clothing and recreation; the right of every farmer to raise and sell his products at a return which will give him and his family a decent living; the right of every businessman, large and small, to trade in an atmosphere of freedom from unfair competition and domination by monopolies at home and abroad; the right of every family to a decent home; the right to adequate medical care and the opportunity to achieve and enjoy good health; the right to adequate protection from the economic fears of old age, sickness, accident and unemployment; the right to a good education. "All of these rights spell security. And after this war is won we must be prepared to move forward, in the implementation of these rights, to new goals of human happiness and well-being."

If the counterattack develops static obstinacy against these rights, the end of the war with Japan will find the promises given for sacrifice confronting the sacrificers of promises. Two opposed obstinacies would be bad for democracy. It will not, it is to be hoped, turn out that these promises were merely toys lent to the children during a time of illness or fairy tales told during a fever.

Long-term and profound anxieties have been developing in the public mind about the quality of the service rendered by industry to modern society. Essentially, but not exclusively, those anxieties issued from the great depression and the deficiencies of the competitive system. It may seem almost obscene to raise again the outcry of all those who suffered from mass unemployment, but it is important once again to draw attention to it. For the very same song that many economists croaked between 1929 and the war is beginning again: that if things are let alone, then *in the long run* there will be a return to "equilibrium"; that, if the market and wages and prices are allowed to take their own natural course, all will be well. But it is not alone those who had employment to lose who have become disaffected, it is also those who had homes, savings, educational opportunity, businesses, and other such things to lose, and lost them. They, too, can no longer believe in the merits of private enterprise alone to satisfy economic needs.

The reaction had already begin in the 'thirties. The New

Deal stuck in conservative throats, although the issue by then was almost that of saving our whole system from revolution. Indeed, Mrs. Sidney Webb asked me, "Would it not have been better for America if there had been no Franklin D. Roosevelt and no New Deal?" For then, she believed, there would have been a revolution; and it would have been interesting to watch the social results — to see whether the United States was as virile as the U.S.S.R. or as decadent as Great Britain!

These were the years of *Assignment in Utopia* by Eugene Lyons, and of W. H. Chamberlin's *Collectivism — A False Utopia*. They reacted from Russia, from the Nazis and from the Fascists. At the same time, they were so unmeasured that they also reacted against the firm course of reform of an economic system whose inefficiencies were many, and for which feasible administrable democratic remedies were known. In revulsion from government by dictatorial minorities, they also became sour towards majority rule. Hayek is the lineal descendant of these.

Then, and even more so now after years of sacrifice, there were "giant evils" to be fought. In Sir William Beveridge's words: "Reconstruction has many sides, international and domestic. On the domestic side one can define its aims best by naming five giant evils to be destroyed — Want, Disease, Ignorance, Squalor and Idleness." [1]

Now I do not wish to be saddled with — I here repudiate — advocacy of a planned economy without qualification, or advocacy of the Russian economy and political system as it is. I disavow these. Let there be no mistake about this. If I am a "socialist," it is in the British sense, where democracy is first and socialism second, as will amply appear. But it is essential that all who are interested in maintaining the Democratic State should realize that the most serious atten-

[1] Address, July 30, 1942. *Cf. Pillars of Security* (London, 1942), p. 42.

tion must be given to the fulfillment of wartime promises, and to the abatement of the abuses of the prewar system of private enterprise — that is to say, its tendency to depressions, its poverty and miseries, its injustices, its inadequacy in bringing about greater abundance. To come along at this critical time, as Mr. Hayek does, and ascribe to "a" system of economic planning all the degenerate consequences of three alien, totalitarian regimes — the Nazi, the Fascist, and the Communist — and to be able with this travesty in mind to win a hearing among thousands upon thousands, and to be supported by periodicals and newspapers, is a sinister event.[2] For it shows that forces of unreason have been straining at the leash, waiting to help history to make a book!

No one intends to "plan" or "collectivize" or "socialize" *all* economic activities, but many do wish to administer solid remedies to an admittedly defective order. Hayek allows no refuge, however, to the moderate person. He does not *let* you be moderate: it spoils his theory! Thus: —

> If we are, nevertheless, rapidly moving toward such a state (of complete centralization which still appalls most people), this is largely because most people still believe that it must be possible to find some middle way between "atomistic" competition and central direction. Nothing, indeed, seems at first more plausible, or is more likely to appeal to reasonable people, than the idea that our goal must be neither the extreme decentralization of free competition nor the complete centralization of a single plan, but some judicious mixture of the two methods. Yet mere common sense proves a treacherous guide in this field. Although competition can bear some admixture of regulation, it cannot be combined with

[2] *Cf. Fortune,* June 1945.

planning to any extent we like without ceasing to operate as an effective guide to production.[3]

He says that a planner cannot avoid planning more than is intended; for every feature which is planned is intertwined with some other economic feature that he knows not of, because his brains are not adequate to omniscience, and so the whole becomes planned. And this is "total," and the dictatorship is built. In fact, there is hardly anything that the state should do: for action by the state interferes with a delicate and intricate process whereby the interests of each man automatically intermesh with the rest, as he buys and sells and manufactures and grows produce and moves hither and thither in search of work. And, of course, the sum of the individuals' activities makes up the good of society. Touch this process (Lippmann calls it the "division of labor") at any point, do anything but provide the conditions under which this atomistic system may operate, and you are sliding down the slippery slope to dictatorship.

Many have already accepted the first alternative set forth by him in his ultimatum: "There is no other possibility than either the order governed by the impersonal [!] discipline of the market or that directed by the will of a few individuals." (Page 199.) By focusing the mind on the fictitious horrors of "planning is dictatorship," you take it off the errors of private enterprise. His attack on planning is so intensely bitter because of his secret anguish that his businessman will not act as the "economic man."

[3] Friedrich A. Hayek, *The Road to Serfdom*, pp. 41–42.

# CHAPTER III

# Lunacy about Planning

It is one thing to show a man that he is in
error, and another to put him in possession of truth.
— JOHN LOCKE, *Essay concerning
Human Understanding*

Planning, to Friedrich A. Hayek, is not merely the
planning which may come in the form of the state's positive
economic and social managerial initiative. He supports competitive free enterprise as "planning" — that is, as a means
which society has of bringing about what he calls "the coin-
cidence of individual ends." He is grieved to think that the
other kind of planners, not his kind, have usurped a good
word, which only he and his friends deserve.

It is possible successfully to plan in a fully democratic
society enjoying the plenitude of civil rights, and retain
democracy and the rights. To Hayek and those who now
waltz with him, this thought is abhorrent. Men of property
do not think planning is *desirable;* and so make the gesture
of proving, additionally, that planning is *impossible,* except
at costs which they must paint as horrible.

There is no authoritative or providential definition of this
term "planning." Hayek does not quote one. Many people
since World War I have talked about planning; and they
have ranged all the way from the planning of a garden, or
a city, or a factory area, to the Five-Year Plans of the Soviet
Union and the Four-Year Plans under the charge of that

perverted Falstaff, Goering.[1] In other words, the term "planning" is related to the purpose of the planner; it is not a constant unvarying idea. In the Soviet Union planning rises to the point where nearly all of the productive resources in the nation are owned by the state, the uses to be made of them are decided by the government, and then fulfilled on the orders of the government. The Soviet people enter and pursue occupations opened to them by government-appointed "higher up" business managers; the government also allocates the capital to each industry, and decides the relationship between how much shall be consumed of the annual produce and how much shall be saved and invested for enhancement of the productive resources and stock piles.

Between the two extremes, Hayek's abstraction of economic individualism and the reality of Soviet planning, an enormous spectrum of plans is possible and advocated by various groups. *It is a question of more, or less;* in *which one* of the many sectors of the economy one would apply a plan; with what *general purpose;* how much it would be supplementary to and how far it would altogether supplant private enterprise. A very few — I repeat, a *very few* — progressives might want the whole of planning, with Russian scope and depth. (In their case the world may dismiss the altogether unreal explanation offered by Hayek — that they are actuated by a lust for power. More probably their first and intense feeling is that the system of economic individualism has not solved the problems of poverty and inequality; that it does not produce and distribute wealth as it should, considering the tremendous capacity available and the potentialities of our resources and technology and powers of organization.)

[1] *Cf.* F. P. Chambers, *The War Behind the War,* Ch. VIII and Ch. XIX; Finer, *Representative Government and a Parliament of Democracy* (1923); Lauterbach, *Economics in Uniform* (1944).

For the purpose of this discussion, a plan may be defined as *a series of well-concerted laws, separate as to substance but integrated and then carried into further detail by a series of rules and orders, made by officials deputed thereto, and controlled by the standards enacted in the statutes and subject to parliamentary or judicial revision or both.* Everybody knows where he is. The discretion and its uses are limited by the statutory definition of purpose and method.

It is, however, indispensable to the reactionary apologia to travesty planning in order to produce a false conviction of its impossibility and undesirability. The method followed is the *reductio ad absurdum*.

First, then, what does Hayek pretend that planning is? At various places it is: "We have in effect undertaken to dispense with the forces which produced unforeseen results and to replace the impersonal and anonymous mechanism of the market by collective and 'conscious' direction of all social forces to deliberately chosen goals." (Pages 20–21.) Who is "we"? That is very important. Is it *all* Americans; *all* Englishmen — the rich, the poor, the middle classes? Or is it a large majority of the people, or a bare majority? Or a minority — large, small, growing, declining? No answer. Does "unforeseen results" include unemployment, monopoly, inequality, ill health, malnutrition? Is it reasonable, and, to be forthright, is it honest to use the terms "'conscious' direction of *all* social forces"? The word "all" begs every question Hayek has still to answer. The economic engineer is shooting economic craps with loaded planning. Hayek proceeds: "It ['the concept of socialism'] may mean, and is often used to describe, merely the ideals of social justice, greater equality, and security, which are the ultimate aims of socialism." (Page 32.)

All honorable men will agree that it is a matter of common sense to anybody who has had any practical experience of politics and government on any level, from Washington or London down to his home-town meeting, or even to one who has confined himself only to his business, or his club, or church, that (*a*) the end determines the means; and (*b*) the ways and means depend on how fully and how quickly it is decided that the end is to be attained, which is an affair of the common will after discussion and vote. Easiness in personal relationships comes from moderation; and moderation is a product of self-limitation and time.

Yet, Hayek proceeds, "In this sense socialism means the abolition of private enterprise, of private ownership of the means of production, and the creation of a system of 'planned economy' in which the entrepreneur working for profit is replaced by a central planning body." (Page 32.) Now, there is no such thing as "socialism" in itself; there are many forms of socialism, and the differences are immense. Some socialists are extremely moderate and gradualist in regard to social control. Some think only in terms of regulation of industry; some want fewer sectors to be regulated, some more; some want nationalization of all the means of production, some want only a moderate amount of nationalization, some none at all but only the regulation of the use of property in a variety of ways; some want administration by the traditional government departments, others by new forms of public corporation; some are more centralist, the overwhelming majority are decentralizers; most exclude an enormous range of the most risky new and speculative business; while some are strictly economic, others believe that Christianity should be fostered, or one of its forms, or a new interpretation of it (and it should be remembered that there are today two hundred interpretations of Christianity); some would like to see new family-unit morals, others not; some want a new status for trade-unions, others believe that the present status of trade-unions, their freedom of bargaining and political activity, should be the basis of whatever

27

new system is to be devised. The gradations are numerous, and the extreme span enormous.

It cannot have escaped Hayek that there are very wide differences of opinion on all these matters among socialists, and that, for example, the British Labour Party as a whole has moved from position to position with the passing of the years and the better comprehension of its own problems. By insisting upon separating the ends from the means, Hayek can insinuate that *if there is the means* — that is, a central planning agency — it may then be used for the kind of purposes for which the Nazis built up their dictatorship! All his results are achieved by omitting from account the men who build and direct and manage the systems — whether of economic individualism, or planning. But what kind of economic guidance is it which leaves out the men? It is economics on a blackboard.

John Stuart Mill abhorred the doctrinaire stuff that Hayek utters.

> These philosophers [he meant those like Comte] would have applied and did apply their principles with innumerable allowances. But it is not allowances that are wanted. There is little chance of making due amends in the superstructure of a theory for want of sufficient breadth in its foundation. It is unphilosophical to construct a science out of few agencies by which the phenomena are determined, and leave the rest to the routine of practice or the sagacity of conjecture. . . .[2]

Then Mill observes how necessary it is to have a Science of Character of the various societies without which the branches of social science are imperfect. The science of character would be a "theory of the causes which determine the type of character belonging to a people or an age."[3]

[2] *Logic*, Bk. VI.
[3] *Ibid.*, Bk. II, 487.

In political economy, *for instance,* empirical laws of human nature are tacitly assumed by English thinkers, which are calculated only for Great Britain and the United States. Among other things an intensity of competition is constantly supposed, which, as a general mercantile fact, exists in no country in the world except these two.[4] An English political economist . . . has seldom learned that men, in conducting the business of selling their goods over the counter, should care more about their ease or their vanity than about their pecuniary gain.

I have quoted Mill simply so that we may have on record a voice in the great English tradition: that the character of peoples is to be taken into account in answering questions of political probability. The spirit of the government is omitted from Hayek's study of it; yet all the men on whom he calls for theoretical support looked first to the spirit: so John Locke (the mentor of the Declaration of Independence); so, above all, Montesquieu — who sought in the machinery of government such a play on the temper of men and in the temper of men such a tension on the machinery that they might be governed *by the laws suited to their condition,* and not by arbitrary power unsanctioned by laws made by the legislature. Hayek cannot do this, for then he would let himself in for a comparison of the spirit of economic individualism and the spirit of socialism, which is to be discovered not by deductive reasoning such as he employs, but by observation. John Stuart Mill did observe, and finally concluded, that the good of England required socialism.[5] Hayek does not mention that.

He and the reactionaries prefer to say, "Although to most

[4] Mill was writing in 1843!
[5] *Cf. Autobiography,* Columbia University Press, 1924, 162–164.

socialists only one species of collectivism will represent true socialism, it must always be remembered that socialism is a species of collectivism and that therefore everything which is true of collectivism as such must apply also to socialism." (Pages 33–34.) The use of the word *true* is entirely gratuitous, and it is exactly like the use of the words "true," "pure," and "real," which German and Austrian philosophers, long before Hayek, employed to distinguish what they wanted a thing to mean as distinct from what the common-sense observation of events and analysis of their meaning show us that they do mean.

Who says what "collectivism" is? No one, except Hayek, and he is hardly disinterested. Is it the "collectivism" of Robert Owen, or Karl Marx, or Saint-Simon, or Fourier, or Lenin, or Sidney and Beatrice Webb, or Eduard Bernstein, or Norman Thomas? He does not say. He is not interested in differences and distinctions, though he claims that freedom of choice is morality, and he disregards the teaching of Aristotle, the greatest political and ethical master of all times, who pointed out that the capacity for distinction differentiates the human being from the brutes. Is the species different according to different countries? J. S. Mill, full of good sense, urged the need of a special science to reveal the relationship between the character of different countries and their institutions, of which socialism would be one. Is the species different, and, if so, for what reasons, in Russia, Great Britain, and the United States? Of course it is; and for reasons which it should have been the urgent duty of Hayek and his anti-Russian claque to follow through for the sake of candor.

He is shaking off all moderation, for like all revolutionaries, even reactionaries, it is his purpose to make you choose between two extremes. So he slides in the word "regimentation" as equal to socialism and planning. (Page 34.) And then he lets himself go. "What our planners demand is a

30

central direction of all economic activity according to a single plan, laying down how the resources of society should be 'consciously directed' to serve particular ends in a definite way." (Page 35.) This leads to the identification of "collectivism, communism, fascism, etc.," in organizing "the whole of society and all its resources for this unitary end and in refusing to recognize autonomous spheres in which the ends of the individuals are supreme. In short they are *totalitarian* . . . which we have adopted to describe the unexpected but nevertheless inseparable manifestations of what in theory we call collectivism." (Pages 56–57. Italics mine.)

Thus, "planning" is "socialism," it is "collectivism," it is "communism," it is "fascism," and it is "totalitarian." The species and the genus have now been confounded.

It is perfectly easy now for Hayek to attribute the ends and the methods of any sort of dictatorship to planning, for totalitarianism and dictatorship have been identified in our own time. Hence planning is dictatorship. Dictatorship is German Nazism especially; then Italian Fascism, and Russian Communism. Hence the United States and Great Britain will soon be like Germany, Italy, and Russia. But, indeed, it is only Hayek's conception of planning which is undesirable and impossible, not the reality of planning which the men and the groups and the electorates who are actually interested in planning desire to see enacted and administered.

Planning, says Hayek, is dictatorship and totalitarianism, because it cannot be controlled by a democracy. If "conscious control" is sought by society in the name of one single goal over every end that man can imagine, then "conscious control" is not manageable by democracy. Then he proceeds with the argument as though the word *if* were not there.

The nature of a government, however, depends upon its purposes, upon who develops it, the terms in which its purpose is stated, the conditions attached to their fulfillment,

31

and, above all, upon *where the authority rests*. Is the government one deputed to do a job by the authority of and with continuing responsibility to the people, or is it an alien body which has usurped power? This fundamental question is ignored by Hayek. He forgets that today, and for many a century past, all that is done by anybody in society is done by the sufferance of society. For society consists of more than a willing buyer and a willing seller. Hayek assumes a *single* purpose and "a complete ethical code in which all the different human values are allotted their due places." (Page 57.) Thus, " 'the social goal,' or 'common purpose,' for which society is to be organized is usually vaguely described as the 'common good,' the 'general welfare,' or the 'general interest.' " (Page 57.) Most would agree that the object of the economic system is the common good, or the general welfare, or, in Jeremy Bentham's phrase, "the greatest happiness of the greatest number."

"The common good," or something like it, is an extremely general phrase, and it was the starting point of Aristotle's *Politics*. Aristotle was sufficiently broad-minded and candid to see and say that there are many different kinds of government adapted to so large a goal. What is the *single* principle to which any planner has committed himself? I do not know of anyone who has made so sweeping a claim as to submerge all individual values or to direct everything. I hate Fascism, Nazism, and Communism, but none of them in fact came anywhere near this sweeping statement of Hayek's, and no planner in any democratic society would accept a totalitarian end. But if Hayek's supposition (*and it is nothing more*) were carried through, it still would not mean either dictatorship or the complete determination of all ethical ends and choices, as set out by him, *provided that its machinery were democratic* — that is to say, so long as its operators were appointed by, or at the behest of, a legislature freely and periodically elected, and changed, by the people. For in that elective process they would be judging the purposes of the plan, and the merits of the men and the measures to carry it out, and the question of repudiating them and choosing other ways and other legislators and executives.

He further maintains that planning will produce the defeat of morality. For, being total, it must require a complete ethical code defining what is right and wrong on everything. Where all the means to be used are the property of society, and are to be used in the name of society according to a unitary plan, "a 'social' view about what ought to be done must guide all decisions. In such a world we should soon find that our moral code is full of gaps." (Pages 57–58.) Yet the code of the world of economic individualism, also, is fearfully full of gaps, and sinister ones; and those who wish to plan economic life better than it is planned today are not concerned with the control of everybody and everything — they are concerned with the serious gaps.

Hayek pretends to think that modern society is getting less and less subject to fixed ethical rules. The manner in which he states his belief is interesting, because it enables us to reveal what the truth actually is. He says: —

It may merely be pointed out that up to the present the growth of civilization has been accompanied by a steady diminution of the sphere in which individual actions are bound by fixed rules. The rules of which our common moral code consists have progressively become fewer and more general in character. From the primitive man, who was bound by an elaborate ritual in almost every one of his daily activities, who was limited by innumerable taboos, and who could scarcely conceive of doing things in a way different from his fellows, morals have more and more tended to become merely limits circumscribing the sphere within which the individual could behave as he liked. The adoption of a common ethical code comprehensive enough to determine a unitary economic plan would mean a complete reversal of this tendency.[6]

It would be useless for Hayek to go back for support before 1776, the date of Adam Smith's *Wealth of Nations,* because then European and British society was mercantilist; that is, the state was a heavy regulator of trade as well as a wide controller of morals and religion. But even later, from Bentham's utility theory of "the greatest happiness of the greatest number" (assumed in the *Fragment on Government,* published in 1776 also), American and British society piled law on law for the advantage of various sections of society; and for the merchant interests in the United States a constitution was created binding the legislature even more than the people. Look how slipshod is the phrase "limited by innumerable taboos"! Bound more than a poor man in Massachusetts in 1789 or 1830?

Professor Hayek's history is not history. Especially before the nineteenth century, but quite plentifully since the sixteenth century, legislation has more and more replaced the growth of custom as the regulator of morals in society in every sphere. Let Professor Hayek read the history of the English Poor Law, for example, from 1535 onwards. Hayek should remember that even the status of the Churches was and is in both the United States and Great Britain regulated by statute or constitution. In every field of individual and social life legislation embodies morals: marriage, divorce, duty to family, religion, property, theft, libel, slander, contract, business — the list is never-ending. This legislation does not come out of the blue, produced without

[6] Hayek, *The Road to Serfdom,* p. 58.

careful reflection and weighing of choices. Hayek must know that.

The accretion of conventions casual and vague in bygone ages is now more deliberate and rational. That is because our society is different in nature, has different ends and a different way of earning its living; it is more complex altogether. It is also not a slave of ignorance of nature and technology, as earlier societies were. It is therefore far more sharply conscious of itself and its possibilities. There is no virtue in worshiping the past on the wrong grounds.

The real difference between the past and the present as regards morality is that the process of making law, that is, the transformation of the developing morality into legislation, is now, in many countries, in the hands *of the whole community*. That is the true distinction between the past, with its priests and medicine men and forbidden apples and more latterly its robber barons, and the present. The process of converting morality into law is democratic, and it is gradual; and it is gradual because it is democratic. Professor Hayek does not disclose this fact or use it in the process of his argument.

Naturally, when Hayek has got so far, he cannot avoid trotting out that ancient nag which is also the steed on which his countryman, Ludwig von Mises, makes many a cavalry skirmish into the camp of the enemy: namely, to show that since all planning begins with one clear conscious objective of an urgent nature, it is to be equated with Military Regimentation. Most people have an idea of what regimentation means. They are then able to argue that, of course, it is the kind of thing we all tolerate during a war, for the defense of our liberties, but, as we would never accept this for economic welfare, as defined by a government for us, then that government would be compelled to take drastic measures against its own citizens, and secure efficient performance by draconic coercion. It may be that, since Hayek was born and bred in Austria, and the best part of his life was therefore spent under an oppressive and bureaucratic and inefficient monarchy, he cannot really understand a people giving itself its own laws and governing themselves without masters, whether aristocrats or the moneyed bourgeoisie. But they do, and can.

This brings us to what is a necessary part, indeed of the very essence of his argument: the idea *that democracy is dangerous and ought to be limited*. It is inevitable that Hayek should be an antagonist of democracy as the consequence of his obsessional attachment to economic individualism. Every successful act of government is a refutation of his planning-is-dictatorship creed. It has been heard before in business circles: "The best government is the worst government!"

Hayek argues that democratic government may act "arbitrarily," and therefore become "dictatorial." To avoid this hypothetical dictatorial result the use of power by democracy must be guided by fixed rules. Of course, they would have to be rules which it could not amend. This is the way in which his mind works on the subject of democracy. (Page 70 and 71.) *He* will not make a fetish of it, for he is more interested in the values that it serves than in itself. He restricts its meaning arbitrarily to, "Democracy is essentially a means, a utilitarian device for safeguarding internal peace and individual freedom." (If it is only a means, what warrant is there for immediately inserting an end?) In other words, it need not accomplish anything, by way of legislation, if the democrats so decide; he neglects its first meaning that it is government by the people. "As such it is by no means infallible or certain. . . . There has often been much more cultural and spiritual freedom under an autocratic rule than under some democracies." This compares unlike with unlike: where was there spirit-

36

ual freedom under an autocracy, and compared with what democracies? No answer. Is the argument applicable to the American and British democracies? No. Again, "Planning leads to dictatorship because dictatorship is the most effective instrument of coercion and the enforcement of ideals and, as such, essential if central planning on a large scale is to be possible." (Page 70.) There might be a "dictatorship of the proletariat" in the interests of the plan; but even if this were "democratic in form," it would destroy personal freedom, and personal freedom is economic freedom, and that freedom is democracy because democracy is "a means for safeguarding internal peace and individual freedom."

The answer is, that if a dictatorship were democratic in form, it could not be a dictatorship; for the democratic form includes instruments and procedures which make it incompatible in action and temper with dictatorship. The only meaning we can attach to this piece of perverted and pompous logic is that if any democracy does not do what Hayek thinks is required in the name of economic individualism it is a dictatorship.

Why should he imagine that millions of individuals running a democracy should be more arbitrary than millions running the economic system on the principle of "individualism"? He attempts to overcome this consideration by further expression of mistrust in democratic government. "The fashionable concentration on democracy . . ." (This phrase — "fashionable" — in England, where they executed a king three hundred years ago and have not slackened in effort for three centuries to attain popular sovereignty; or in the United States, to which men fled from monarchies and fought the War of Independence and the Civil War with democracy on their lips!) ". . . as the main value threatened is not without danger. It is largely responsible for the misleading and unfounded belief that, so long as the

37

ultimate source of power is the will of the majority, the power cannot be arbitrary; . . . the contrast suggested by the statement is altogether false; it is not the source but the *limitation of power which prevents it from being arbitrary.*" (Page 71. The italics are mine.)

He cannot trust in the people, without limitation; nor in the authority of the majority; nor in the people as the source of power. Yet in Great Britain and in the United States democracy, with its ultimate reliance upon the will of the majority, is the product of at least three hundred years of severe mental labor, careful reflection, and piece by piece development. Most of its secrets have been discovered en route; and one of them, which is only one, and represents the spirit in which democracy has come to be worked, is that "liberty is secreted in the interstices of procedure." That happens to be a quotation from Sir Henry Maine, who is the source of a different quotation which is later abused by Hayek.

Democracy in reality consists of procedures, and they are such as to provide for steady reflection, to compel attention to argument, to proceed to legislation deliberately, to allow for amendment, to subject the executive to investigation. There are many others of the same nature. Why should it be assumed that this complex, delicately dovetailed but tensile piece of machinery does not exist? It is decidedly a matter for the highest congratulation that democracies have made a fetish of democracy; there is no reason to sneer about its being "fashionable"! This, in fact, is the only safeguard of that "liberalism" which Hayek says he wants. Once mankind has become conscious of its own political power, there is no other conceivable guarantee. It is wrong to draw a false picture of the parliamentary process under democracy, and to implant a suspicion that even this will disappear, unless cogent reasons are advanced for the proposition. This would be to ape Karl Marx's tactics, that is to say, to sow the idea that the state is the offspring of class warfare and will inevitably be overcome by the sheer inevitable triumph of economic forces.

Hayek guys the parliamentary process; not that of the United States but Great Britain's, which, as all students of comparative institutions are aware, is more mature than that of the United States. The people, he asserts, will have adopted "a system of directed economy" on the plea that it will produce great prosperity. The goal will, in the discussion preceding the legislation, have been described by some such term as "common welfare." (Page 61.) But in fact, as the discussions on postwar economic and social reconstruction down to the recent general election in Great Britain, the Wagner-Murray-Dingall social security and Kilgore full employment bills show, the party programs have been thoroughly elaborated in the greatest detail by intra-party discussion and amendment and reconciliation among the many interests that are domesticated in each political party, before they are put forward to the electorate in considerable particularity. Even in America the Presidential election of November 1944 showed a noticeable agreement on many such subjects of Republicans and Democrats, with the exception of certain "die-hards" who largely compose Hayek's school of thought.

Consider the list at the recent British general election. The Conservative Party submitted a platform on domestic affairs including the maintenance of a high and stable level of employment, with emphasis on free enterprise; a chance for the small man in industry; possible state co-ordination of the coal industry, certainly much control; assistance to all forms of transport; the reduction of taxation; much housing by both public and private enterprise; assistance to agriculture so that more food may be grown than formerly; the fulfillment of the promises of the government of a wide and important social security system based on the insurance principle; a state medical service for all; wide educational opportunity; stimulation of industrial research; regulation of monopolies. The Labour Party proposed to nationalize the coal mines, the iron and steel industry, fuel and power; to regulate banking heavily, to give full social security, full employment, a national health scheme, housing and education in greater measure than the other parties, and, when necessary, to take over monopolies otherwise unmanageable.

This discussion is not, as can be realized, merely about means but about ends. It would be ridiculous for any party to come forward with the demand for what a Conservative Prime Minister, Mr. Baldwin, once called "a doctor's mandate." This is worth noting, for the parties must reconcile all their own internal groups.

Altogether reckless about these facts, Hayek persists in his blindness: "Agreement [within and among the parties] will in fact exist only on the mechanism to be used." Then, if agreement takes place, they will soon find that they are in disagreement about ends. According to Hayek, when this disagreement is discovered, "we cannot confine collective action to the tasks on which we can agree but are forced [*by what compulsion?*] to produce agreement on everything in order that any action can be taken at all." This "is one of the features which contributes more than most to determining the character of a planned system." (Pages 61–62.) If responsibility of mind means the testing of what one imagines by the experience of the senses, and by logically controlled thinking, then Hayek is entirely irresponsible. For experience should show that if a government could not agree on what it was to do, in democratic procedure it would postpone action till its course was decided by submission of the question to the will of the people. There is nothing in Hayek's argument to show why or when any different practice would be adopted.

All that then follows from what Hayek has postulated of planning is vitiated by this nonsensical travesty on how democratic peoples arrive at decisions. It may be said that a vast code of laws on the economy, health, property, civil behavior, relationship of groups to the state, local and central government, the utilities, and — the list would be unending — has been established in the United States and England, all by the democratic process as we have described it, and the nations flourish more than ever, and there is more freedom than ever. Yet Hayek tries to make our flesh creep by arguing that legislatures will never be able to agree on a plan and therefore there will be dissatisfaction with representative legislatures and with democracy, because parliaments will be seen to be only "talking shops"; the conviction will grow then that ". . . if efficient planning is to be done, the direction must be 'taken out of politics' and placed in the hands of experts — permanent officials or independent autonomous bodies." (Page 62.)

It is indeed generally desired to take the "direction" — meaning the administrative management — out of politics, in the sense that the United States Department of Agriculture or Justice or Labor or Civil Service Commission or the T.V.A. or Bonneville Dam is taken out of politics, that all the great public service agencies are taken out of politics: so that the internal technical problems which are naturally involved in operation may be properly considered, leaving the purpose and direction and responsible controls in political hands.

Hayek and his friends would be the first to sneer if this sort of "taking out of politics" were not done or proposed in government planning. Nearly a century of effort in England has contributed to this purging of partisan favoritism from public management; in the United States merit and the exclusion of "spoils" and patronage and partisan bias have evolved with marked rapidity and success since 1883.

All are to be praised that a democracy has been able to appreciate the need for objective nonpartisan management, and that it has been developed with perhaps a greater degree of success than that which competition has achieved in separating family and other favoritism from the technical considerations of economic service.

So also of the "autonomous bodies" referred to, perhaps bodies like the government corporations in the United States and in Great Britain. The invention of this form of administration is one of the greatest moment, for it has two advantages: the first is to expel partisan considerations from management of public utilities; the second is to free the management from certain traditional bonds of procedure now found to be unnecessary and trammeling, and functionally bad. Both of these were the discoveries of people interested in making democratic economic and social action by government — that is, planning — at once more inventive and more responsible, and not subject to being debauched by any group that could get its finger into the administration.

Hayek can only batter down the idea of government planning by the majority by capriciously stipulating that majorities are supposed to "produce agreement on everything," and when Hayek says everything, he means *everything*. (Page 64.) Who ever asked that? Has any law ever had a unanimous acceptance? Has society ever agreed unanimously on all laws at the same time, before it has voted acceptance of any one law? The majority is not something that suddenly appears in the legislature out of the blue. It is the result of an election, and the election is the end result of a long process of preparation. The majority in the legislature makes the law, but the people have made that majority and have defined what that majority may do. If the majority outside and inside the legislature cannot decide, then the matter is not decided, but is postponed on

42

the basis of the maximum agreement that can immediately be reached. Subsequently, by a process of further argument and study and wrangling, the issue will be determined one way or another. The only way that Hayek can get around this is to deny the right of sovereignty to the majority. And, of course, that is what he does.

Hayek's unscrupulous travesty of the democratic process of securing legislation (for that is the first basis of any government plan) culminates in his general contempt for the democratic notion altogether. This passage is so extraordinary that it must be quoted in full: —

> We must not deceive ourselves into believing that all good people must be democrats or will necessarily wish to have a share in the government. Many, no doubt, would rather intrust it to somebody whom they think more competent. Although this might be unwise, there is nothing bad or dishonorable in approving a dictatorship of the good.[7]

This, decidedly, is not the spirit of American or British democracy. It is its deadly and poisonous enemy. This infamous, malignant outlook is precisely what subverted the thinly rooted democracies of the Continent. The British spirit of democracy is reflected in the phrase "Good government is no substitute for self-government." The American equivalent is John Adams's "Where annual election ends, tyranny begins."

Hayek concludes his *fausse bonhomie* by this dubious statement: —

> No doubt an American or English "Fascist" system would greatly differ from the Italian or German models; no doubt, if the transition were effected without vio-

[7] *Op. cit.*, p. 134.

lence [How could it be?], we might expect to get a better type of leader. And, if I had to live under a Fascist system, I have no doubt that I would rather live under one run by Englishmen or Americans than under one run by anybody else.[8]

What Englishman or American would speak in this way?

[8] *Op. cit.,* p. 135.

# CHAPTER IV

# The Rule of Law Is the Rule of Hayek

> Neither is God appointed and confined, where and out of what place these his chosen shall be first heard to speak.
>
> — JOHN MILTON, *Areopagitica*

It is only a seeming paradox that men with the temper of Hayek and his entourage should begin with "economic individualism" and end by proposing to appropriate the nation's constitution. This ambition has been manifested with special clarity in the long-term attitude of the conservatives to the judgments of the United States Supreme Court in "due process" cases. It was altogether in this spirit that when I was speaking to a Rotary Club a member interrupted and declared: "There is no Supreme Court." When I answered that the Court was actually in session and handing down judgments, it became clear that the heckler meant that the judges were no longer giving conservative judgments, therefore there was no Supreme Court or Constitution!

Hayek takes exactly the same position, but wraps it up in many technicalities, which we must now lay bare. Briefly, he exploits the most noble notion of the Rule of Law for ignoble ends; and in doing so is obliged to pervert terms and ideas whose significance is well-established among political scientists.

The term Rule of Law was used by the English constitutional jurist, A. V. Dicey, in his *Introduction to the Study of the Law of the Constitution,* first published in 1885 and now in its ninth edition: —

> When we say that the supremacy or the rule of law is a characteristic of the English constitution, we generally include under one expression at least three distinct though kindred conceptions. We mean, in the first place, that no man is punishable or can be lawfully made to suffer in body or goods except for a distinct breach of law established in the ordinary legal manner before the ordinary courts of the land. In this sense the rule of law is contrasted with every system of government based on the exercise by persons in authority of wide, arbitrary, or discretionary powers of constraint. . . . We mean, in the second place . . . not only that with us no man is above the law, but (what is a different thing) that here every man, whatever be his rank or condition, is subject to the ordinary law of the realm and amenable to the jurisdiction of the ordinary tribunals. . . . The "rule of law," lastly, may be used as a formula for expressing the fact that with us the law of the constitution, the rules which in foreign countries[1] naturally form part of a constitutional code, are not the source but the consequence of the rights of individuals, as defined and enforced by the courts; that, in short, the principles of private law[2] have with us been by the action of the courts and Parliament so extended as to determine the position of the Crown and of its servants; thus the constitution is the result of the ordinary law of the land.

Much of the rest of Dicey's treatise is devoted to the

[1] Dicey thinks almost entirely of Europe, and often of the eighteenth century.

[2] As distinguished from the Continental "public law," constitutional and administrative law.

demonstration that Parliament, the lawmaking body, is supreme over everybody and everything. Indeed, he was the inventor of the phrase that Parliament can do anything except change a man into a woman.

Now Dicey's purpose was to distinguish British parliamentary sovereignty, and *under it* judicial supremacy, over all things and all men in the land, from the Continental constitutions, just emerging from autocracy. Nothing was further from his mind than to teach that Parliament itself was subject to any authority, least of all a written constitution outside. His first point, relating to the use of discretionary power, was directed against the practice which allowed European executives a large customary traditional power of making decrees, sovereign in authority; and his point about the "ordinary" law courts related to the existence in European countries of specialized courts, inside and outside the government departments, which settled disputes between the government and individuals or corporations. There is nothing more in it than that. He did not detract one iota from the British principle of the supremacy of Parliament, and it is within this supremacy that the Rule of Law operates.

Omitting any explanation to his readers that the law and even the constitution itself is in English theory and practice the product of Parliament, where the majority is master, Hayek most cunningly and evasively, having used "Rule of Law" for the credit that it gives, says in his footnote: "Largely as a result of Dicey's work the term has, however, in England acquired a narrower technical meaning which does not concern us here." And then he slides away on an elusive and vague remark about the "wider and older meaning of *the concept* of the rule or *reign* of law"; and says this was discussed in the nineteenth century in Germany, when the Germans discussed the nature of the *Rechtstaat!* Notice, a *concept* is his cloudy refuge! But what was the *Rechtstaat* idea in Germany? When in the nineteenth century (*circa* 1825–1875) German liberals or democrats, of the upper classes (the masses did not count at all), wished to liberalize their ancient and inveterately absolute monarchy with its two-century-old assistant bureaucracy, the least that they could claim, as they could not possibly get a popular and responsible system of government based on representation, like that of the English and the Americans, was that the royal officials should conduct their administration only subject to suit in the courts to determine their authority to utter such decrees and execute them. This was no democratic Rule of Law but only a framework within which the officials could legally operate. That is all the *Rechtstaat* could mean to them.

To Hayek, law does not mean what the legislature enacts. He wants to go behind the legislature and prohibit it from acting except as he thinks fit. All else is arbitrary to him.

Let us look into this: —

> Nothing distinguishes more clearly conditions in a free country from those in a country under arbitrary government than the observance in the former of the great principles known as the Rule of Law. *Stripped of all technicalities,* this means that government in all its actions is bound by rules fixed and announced beforehand — rules which make it possible to foresee with fair certainty how the authority will use its coercive powers in given circumstances and to plan one's individual affairs on the basis of this knowledge . . . the essential point, that the discretion left to the executive organs wielding coercive power should be reduced as much as possible, is clear enough.[3]

[3] Hayek, *The Road to Serfdom,* pp. 72–73. Italics mine. I had hoped to avoid personal reminiscence, but it is impossible in view of Hayek's evasiveness. When he first broached his

When Hayek says "stripped of all technicalities," he is prostituting the very safeguards for which judges and statesmen have fought for 350 years.

Next, Hayek gives the Rule of Law a different meaning altogether. (Page 73. Italics mine.) It is "a permanent framework of laws within which the productive activity is guided by *individual* decisions"; while "arbitrary government" is "the direction of economic activity by a central authority" — that is, it is planning. In other words, the Rule of Law is no other than our old friend competition and, as we shall see later, the Engineer's Clock of Prices, wound up by God, as Leibnitz affirmed, into a "pre-established harmony" among all the individuals and then left alone!

Hayek likes formal rules or laws, and not the kind of rules and laws which a planning authority would make. The latter would make decisions, he thinks, about production: what is to be produced and the number of people to be in an industry, the price of shoes, how many busses are to be run. All these decisions depend on the circumstances of the moment. Hence somebody will have to change the plans for the given task, and since this cannot be done by a representative legislature, there is arbitrary power, and there the Rule of Law does not operate.

Is this not a travesty? First, in the system of the so-called competitive market, there are similar adjustments that must be made to the circumstances of the moment. Second, the managers of state enterprises, or the individuals

---

peculiar personal idea of the Rule of Law and Planning to the author and a few friends some three years ago, all who heard him, being scholars of world repute, immediately denounced his history and citation of the Rule of Law as false. He seems to have tried to escape the true facts by this device of "stripped of all technicalities" — but the Rule of Law is compact of technicality!

and firms being regulated by them (for that is an alternative to full management), would act according to principles settled by the legislature, and elaborated with the assistance of advisory bodies of all interests concerned. Third, these people would be as capable as the economic individualist as he actually works (not as he is supposed to work when a concept in a seminar discussion) in forecasting the changes, and therefore preparing for them. The amount of profit won, the number of fluctuations in losses and bankruptcies, the unpublished settlements with ruined creditors, are signs of the inability of the actual individualist to forecast.[4] Fourth, where certain markets and demands were particularly risky, fluid, and elastic, and concerned luxuries, the planners would probably decide not to exert control at all.

I hold no brief for the Russian system, on which Hayek is unwontedly mum. But it would be foolish to say that it is without law, or that Soviet people cannot forecast what their situation is likely to be.

What Hayek is looking for is something, as he says, which resembles the British Highway Code, laying down the Rule of the Road, rather than laws ordering people where

[4] *Cf.* Report of the Delegation on Economic Depressions of the League of Nations, *Transition from War to Peace Economy,* Part I, pp. 23–24: "During the last twenty years the price of wheat and of jute has been halved three times within about twelve months, the price of cotton three times in periods of under eighteen months. The price of copper and of lead was halved four times within periods of two years and doubled three times even more rapidly. The price of zinc was halved twice in eighteen months; of tin twice in twenty-four months; zinc and lead doubled in price three times in two years or less; copper three times in eighteen months. On one occasion the price of coffee was halved in eight months, on another the price of sugar trebled in four months. Between 1920 and 1933 the price of crude rubber fluctuated between four cents a pound and twenty-five times that amount and was on several occasions doubled or halved in the space of a few months."

they are to go: or better still he looks to the state's providing signposts but not commanding people which road to take. This is the most extreme example which he can choose to illustrate his idea. But, actually Parliament did enact the principles of the Highway Code; the Ministry of Transport under this authority prepared it with the assistance of the automobile and pedestrian and cyclist and other associations; it was thus promulgated, and submitted to Parliament for approval. Certain infringements of it are punishable, and the law courts are continually occupied with offenses under it. The law, in short, does tell people where to go — they cannot go across the road, they must take certain detours and so expend additional gasoline; they cannot go down one-way streets. What the British Highway Code has determined for people is that they must surrender certain of their liberties for two reasons: (*a*) to save other people's lives, limbs, and time; (*b*) to save their own.

Is a law for land drainage admissible? Is a statute establishing land and mineral conservation authorities and prescribing landowners' duties admissible? Is a law establishing Pure Food and Drugs standards, and therefore duties, permissible? A law to regulate the sale of electricity? One establishing schedules of charges for the use of grain elevators, which are strategic points in the agricultural world? Where do these essentially differ from the law prescribing that there shall be an election among workers to choose their labor union? Laws of the latter kind sought to free men from the tyranny of the circumstances of the moment. What is a law against theft? What is a social insurance law? What is a law setting up a service of maternity and child welfare? What is the Fair Labor Standards Act, and what are the laws regarding the safeguarding of workers against dangerous machinery and processes? The knowledge that the state will act in a definite way is precisely the character of all these laws.

There is no way that Hayek can distinguish between the essential nature of different laws. All laws are commands telling people what not to do and what to do; some go into more detail and some into less. They are known in advance; they cannot be known in all detailed applicability to each individual case and they must be interpreted under guarantees of good faith, and by the judges. It is exceptional obtuseness to argue as Hayek does that it is a virtue of competition that we know *less* about the particular effect of measures taken by the state than we would where the state is totally active! Actually, all those who are subject to the practice of competition have ample knowledge of its particular effects: but in many cases they have no authority to cure them, and no one to listen to their complaints and decide whether there is justice or injustice in the situation which calls for remedy.

Hayek demands that the state be impartial (Page 75) among particular people and particular ends. This is a will-o'-the-wisp as his own argument in favor of economic individualism shows. No state that has ever existed has ever been impartial among individuals. It is the definition of a state that it is partial: it stands for a hierarchy of purposes, and it is that or it is not a state. Every law is a declaration of partiality for some group or some object. John Locke, the Whig, would tell him that. All government rests on this foundation. Is it Hayek's object to get rid of government? No, he needs it for his own purposes; that is to say, he and his friends very emphatically want it to be partial to their point of view. Is there to be no state at all, but only the rule of the businessmen, who will possess themselves of it as the British and American mercantilists once did? If there is a state, it operates through legislators and the executive, and it can be demanded of them that it shall be heard in the discussion and creation of the law.

Is it required to limit the state? Hayek and Lippmann

definitely answer, "Yes." How? Popular sovereignty must be limited. Lippmann goes back to the Founding Fathers, mercantilists, not men of *laissez faire,* who wanted to "refine" democracy, in other words, to castrate it, so that the men of property might govern.[5] Hayek says: —

> The idea that there is no limit to the powers of the legislator is in part a result of popular sovereignty and democratic government. It has been strengthened by the belief that, so long as all actions of the state are duly authorized by legislation, the Rule of Law will be preserved. But this is completely to misconceive the meaning of the Rule of Law. This rule has little to do with the question whether all actions of the government are legal in the juridical sense. They may well be and yet not conform to the Rule of Law.[6]

Now this doctrine is the antithesis of the American and British doctrine of democracy. The Rule of Law is not juridical, it is parliamentary. Sovereign power lies in the British Parliament; in the American system in the constitutional disposition of powers and so in the people, acting upon it according to the amending clause.

Hayek takes refuge in something else altogether. He returns to the Rule of Law "as a vague ideal" which "has, however, existed at least since Roman times," and "during the last few centuries it has never been so seriously threatened as it is today." (Page 82.) What is this ideal? Since Hayek does not fully state it, we will. Men, living in society, are obliged to enter into social relations. The millions cannot live as isolated Crusoes. Whatever freedom men may desire none ask for freedom from Justice. Some order,

[5] *Cf.* the brilliant essay by Walton Hamilton, *The Power to Govern.*

[6] Hayek, *op. cit.,* p. 82.

that is a moral relationship, is bound to establish itself between them as the result of their many impulses of association and disassociation, and order means that a hierarchy of values will establish itself. (I leave out of account an alien conqueror.) Are they to have peace, order, tranquillity, welfare; or are they to have theft, lying, constraint, force? Are they to have each his own faith regarding the destiny of man and therefore his rights and duties? Who is to state what these are? Without such a determination life would be intolerably insecure and incalculable. It would be, in Hobbes's famous words, a "war of every man against every man," and its product a life "solitary, poor, nasty, brutish and short."

Hence, since the time that man began to reflect on his problems, he has made attempt after attempt to discover who is the legitimate, the rightful person or group, to declare the obligations and enforce them. Whatever various men have decided on this question — that is, who, and for what, and how far and how deeply the authority of the government shall be and shall go — they have usually ascribed the result of their findings to natural law: they have said that this is to be deduced from surveying nature. Nature, or God, or God in Nature, or Nature in God has been their ultimate justification. To some Nature has meant the contemplation of the Divinity as they have understood Him; to others the more profane survey of the psychology and spirit of man, as revealed in the long process of history, or directly in contemporary action and thought; or some have scanned the future of man through their own wishes and have declared that this and this is natural and divine. Of course, any natural law and natural rights thus discovered are considered by them the supreme law, and everlasting. Cicero has said it for all time: "We are born for justice, and that right is founded not in opinion but in nature. There is, indeed, a true law, right reason, agreeing with

54

nature and diffused among all, unchanging, everlasting. . . . It is not allowable to alter this law or to deviate from it, nor can it be abrogated. Nor can we be released from this law either by the Senate or by the people." *This* then determines who shall rule legitimately, and the utterances of this authority for the purposes mentioned and by the standards limited are good law. All the rest is arbitrary. Hayek means this; and Hayek is doing likewise. He is searching for natural law and natural rights derived from that law, and that is what he calls the Rule of Law. This, however, is entirely subjective, and ought not to be connected with any pretense of being based on the Rule of Law as the term is used in the law of England.

So Hayek moves towards his unamendable constitution. There must be "rules previously laid down"; and (Page 83) the Rule of Law could not be preserved "in a democracy that undertook to decide every conflict of interests not according to rules previously laid down but 'on its merits.'" It may be rejoined that the statutes of Congress and the laws of Parliament are rules previously laid down. No! He does not mean this. "The Rule of Law thus implies limits to the scope of legislation. . . . It means not that everything is regulated by law, but, on the contrary, that the coercive power of the state *can be used only in cases defined in advance by the law* and in such a way that it can be foreseen how it will be used. A particular enactment can thus infringe the Rule of Law." (Pages 83–84. Italics mine.) There must be rules in advance of the statutes. He (like Lippmann) wants the legislature limited in its powers. "Whether, as in some countries, the main applications of the Rule of Law are laid down in a bill of rights or in a constitutional code, or whether the principle is merely a firmly established tradition, matters comparatively little. But it will readily be seen that, whatever form it takes, any such recognized limitations of the powers of legislation imply the recognition of the inalienable right of the individual, inviolable rights of man." (Page 84.)

Now, this necessitates a written law, not mere traditional restraints. If we rely on tradition only, many holders of property rights will seriously abuse their powers. That destroys tradition. Are other men to fight back and take the enclosed land away; jump other people's claims; kill a thief of bequests; thrash the vendor of tainted ham that gives ptomaine poisoning; destroy dangerous machinery; set fire to banks that have gambled away a grocer's deposits; derail the trains whose owners practise discriminatory rates? Or are men in so complex a society to proceed by the orderly making of law, lest tradition be forgotten or mocked? Is it to be punishment and indemnities, if collectible, after injury or ruin, or perhaps death, or is it to be preventive action? If they decide the latter, which is a marvel of self-restraint, who is to make the law and by what procedure? A lawmaking body, and the majority? There is no way out of this, short of ascribing legitimacy to a minority. Therefore the guarantees of Hayek's principles must take the form of a bill of rights which cannot be amended, for if it is amendable, even by a qualified majority, then, sooner or later, society, under pressure of distress, will amend that bill of rights.

If the Constitution is unamendable, who is the interpreter of the bill of rights? The words used by Hayek, "the inalienable right of the individual, inviolable rights of man," are vague; and, even if put down in the far more detailed form of the amendments to the United States Constitution, are subject to enormous elasticity by interpretation. Does he know anything of the fate of bills of rights under the United States Constitution? Does he realize that some 30,000 cases have been fought since 1789 on the meaning to be attached to the Constitution, and that specifically for interpretation of the so-called Bill of Rights and the clauses

56

of General Welfare, of Due Process, of Taxation, thousands have been fought; and that as a result there has been a tremendous change in the law under the impulse of changes in society and its economy and its state of mind? There has developed such relative fluidity that men like the leader writers of the *Chicago Tribune* believe there is no longer a Constitution.

But what is the answer to this problem? The judges are independent; but someday they will die, and then there must be a new appointment. Who is to appoint? The representatives of the majority party? If the representatives of the majority party appoint them, in the course of time, the Constitution being, as the saying goes, "what the judges say it is," the judges will say what the majority wants, and the Supreme Court will follow the election returns. Hayek does not believe that it is proper for the judges to change their minds under popular influence. Then he should propose a way of appointing justices who can be fully relied on never to change their minds. If there are several judges and not one, how can he avoid their vagaries and their changes of mind and the ambiguity that has come from the fact that men change their minds? It looks as though under Hayek's dispensation one man ought to be judge, and to judge forever. But even that would not do for Hayek's thesis. The eternal judge might, after all effort had been made to avoid it, still change his mind about the meaning of economic individualism and leave men in that state of uncertainty which Hayek so affects to fear when uncertainty comes from the action of the state and not from the action of economic individualists. The only way out of the dilemma, for him, would be for Hayek to be the judge, and to live forever. But he must not be influenced by the theories of Lord Keynes or Sir William Beveridge! He would have to ban men like the Yankee from Olympus, who had so much good sense that he kicked Herbert Spencer's *Social*

*Statics* — a direct predecessor of *The Road to Serfdom* — down the steps of the United States Supreme Court.[7] This is the *self-reductio ad absurdum* of Hayek. He leads to a dictatorship of Hayekian principles.

Having dethroned despotic monarchs and rejected the infallibility of Popes, what case is there for canonizing Hayek? Why should it be given to Hayek alone to force us to be free?

[7] On this there is a now long-famous dictum, to which the United States Supreme Court has done and does homage. It is that of Justice Holmes, in *Lochner* v. *New York* (1905), when the Court five to four (what a commentary on the certainty of economic individualism such decisions are) decided that a ten-hour-day law for bakeries interfered with the liberty of contract — which was deemed to be included in the liberty protected by the 14th Amendment. "This case is decided upon an economic theory which a large part of the country does not entertain. If it were a question whether I agreed with that theory, I should desire to study it further and long before making up my mind. But I do not conceive that to be my duty, because I strongly believe that my agreement or disagreement has nothing to do with the right of the majority to embody their opinions in law. It is settled by various decisions of this court that state constitutions and state laws may regulate life in many ways which we as legislators might think as injudicious or if you like as tyrannical as this, and which equally with this interfere with the liberty to contract. . . . The 14th Amendment does not enact Mr. Herbert Spencer's *Social Statics*. . . .

"A constitution is not intended to embody a particular economic theory, whether of paternalism and the organic relation of the citizen to the State or of *laissez faire*. It is made for people of fundamentally differing views. . . . Every opinion tends to become a law. I think that the word liberty in the 14th Amendment is perverted when it is held to prevent the natural outcome of a dominant opinion, unless it can be said that a rational and fair man necessarily would admit that the statute proposed would infringe fundamental principles as they have been understood by the traditions of our people and our law. . . ."

58

It is not the bill of rights he wants; but that particular bill of rights that will permanently enthrone Hayek's specific economic theories. For example, the Constitution of the Union of Soviet Socialist Republics of the year 1936 contains a Bill of Rights. Would that be satisfactory to Hayek? It satisfies his *formal* prescription. Articles 1 to 12 assert the foundation of a socialist economy, with the means of production in the hands of the society of workers and peasants; allow some personal property and the right of inheritance of this; declare that the economic life of the country is determined and directed by a state plan of national economy in the interests of increasing the public wealth, of steadily raising the material and cultural standard of the working people, of strengthening the independence and defensive capacity of the Union of Soviet Socialist Republics, and of laying down the distributive rule that he who does not work shall not eat. Chapter X contains the Basic Rights and Duties of Soviet Citizens: they guarantee employment, the right to rest, social security, education, freedom of conscience, speech, the press, of assembly and meetings, of association (with the Communist Party as Leader), inviolability of person, of homes, of correspondence. But Hayek, Lippmann, Chamberlin, *et hoc genus omne,* would repudiate it because it does not accord with Hayek's theories of economics. But none of them seizes upon the supreme ground for rejection: that though rights are established, the machinery of governmental responsibility to the people is defective.

Hayek repudiates majority rule. What then remains? We cannot say individualism, in general, remains; because the only guarantee of that, if there can be any, is the rule of the majority which Hayek repudiates. He tries to crown his particular form of anarchy with a hereditary and unassailable crown.

It is one of Hayek's favorite tricks in oral debate on the theme of the Rule of Law, as we have discussed it, to put this truculent question, which he regards as consternation-making and decisive. "If a majority voted a dictator, say Hitler, into power, would that still be the Rule of Law?" Indeed, he puts this question in *The Road to Serfdom*. The answer is Yes; the majority would be right: the Rule of Law would be in operation, *if* the majority *voted* him into power. The majority might be unwise, and it might be wicked, but the Rule of Law would prevail. For in a democracy right is what the majority makes it to be. It is, however, unbelievable that an American or British majority would vote a Hitler into office, for these majorities have their own abilities and modes of thinking and procedures as part of majority rule. Hayek answers his own piece of Ph.D. pedantry thus: "It may well be that Hitler has obtained his unlimited powers in a strictly constitutional manner and that whatever he does is therefore legal in the juridical sense. But who would suggest for that reason that the Rule of Law still prevails in Germany?" (Page 82.) No one would; and no one knowing the facts would say that Hitler had obtained unlimited powers in a strictly constitutional manner.

Hitler was never voted into office by a majority in Germany; the votes he was able to obtain in March 1933 were made possible only by the suspension of the Bill of Rights by the senile President Hindenburg, which enabled Hitler to scatter his opponents *by force*.

There is nothing for it: the majority will have its way. It is inside the majority that the Rule of Law rightly operates. Nowhere else can our trust and hope reside in these centuries of high democratic consciousness. Democracy must be cherished, in order that we may do all to preserve and improve it, this great *vis medicatrix* of society. We individuals are its parts, and all the other individuals are as beholden to us as we to them to keep open the way for the future.

The majority in the United States and Great Britain has used its power with deliberate wisdom. It has begged for and established education, always more and more improved (in England, against the will of the "governing" class). It has established political associations with rules regarding the nomination and selection of candidates for office; for educating their members; for researching into national and local problems; for contesting opposing views with manners and tactics that draw out those views and mitigate error and moderate passions; for controlling legislative representatives, and sending deputations and advisers to the government departments. With passionate and victorious force it has beaten against the earlier restrictions upon the publicity of proceedings in its parliaments and its law courts. It has abolished the laws against freedom of communication. It has reinforced the legislatures so that they survey and penetrate to all parts of the administrative apparatus and process. It has supported the cause of a free press, even when some of those who conducted the free press were men whose views were unpopular. It has encouraged temperate proceedings in its legislatures, and more and more moderated and controlled corrupt practices in elections and parliamentary lobbying. It has supported procedures which assure that public affairs and private businesses whose operations affect the lives of millions shall be thoroughly investigated *subpoena* from time to time. It has favored the development of rules guaranteeing a due consideration for all projects of law from their earliest formative stages, with proper debate, amendment, and the right of the minority not only to a say in the course of debate but to consultation on a basis of democratic reciprocity, and a right of obstruction sufficient to get the point of view of the minority embodied in the law. Finally, it has invented parliamentary comity, so that men may meet on a common floor, where justice may be the object of men-

61

tal strife, not to determine the stronger of one "justice" against another, but to determine which ideas, embodied in the "justice" of each side, can be reconciled in a law which will be the common habitation of compatriots.

These things the majorities have given to themselves, or, where they have come from a past generation, accepted and adapted to contemporary use. They know their own weakness, holding the freedom to use or abuse their own strength, and so they practise self-control, the only guarantee of self-government. To a student of this evolution, from the outside as one great system compared with others in history, and from the inside watching the gradual accretion of knowledge and techniques and instruments, it is clear that the path taken is the path of continual improvement: more self-knowledge, more self-control, more self-government, with the emphasis on both the positive side of government and the free virile feeling of self. On all this the groups with very different interests have agreed.

Hayek cannot see how, in a planned state, groups can settle their differences over the course to be followed when the state is to undertake various business projects. He pretends that in this case it is necessary to leave it to "the discretion of the judge or authority in question" to decide what is "fair and reasonable." This again is hypothetical. The solution depends on how the law of the plan is constructed, and the ability and state of mind of the negotiators in parliament, in the courts, and in regulatory bodies such as the Tariff Commission, the Interstate Commerce Commission, the Federal Communications Commission, and the Securities and Exchange Commission, which are solving problems and building up important experience. But principally it depends on nationwide debate conducted over the course of years, assisted by the sifted results of scientific research and experience. The plan, such as it is, emerges from the majority; and only that emerges from the majority which the majority can thereafter operate. That is the answer to Hayekian obscurantism.

The discussion of the Rule of Law raises the lesser, more technical but still very important issue of what is variously known as "delegated legislation," "administrative law," or "subordinate legislation." Hayek loses no opportunity of making this seem sinister, although in Great Britain a long and deliberate investigation, by citizens of great repute in the law and administration, decisively rejected the charge which a Conservative judge and many businessmen had made against the so-called "New Despotism," and declared that the government departments were guiltless of arbitrary action or abused powers. Substantially the same verdict was given in the United States, by the Reports of the Attorney General's Committee on Administrative Procedure in Government Agencies (1941). These committees have been entirely above any suspicion of favoritism towards the administrative departments, or what Hayek would call "collectivism" against the individual. It is known that with more tasks the state must have more officials; that legislatures must devolve administration, which includes both enforcement and rule-making, to those officials. But it is also clear that the legislatures are perfectly conscious of their own duty to lay down principles clearly and unmistakably, and to establish in each case a regular procedure — investigation; hearing with counsel; recording evidence; taking counsel with the interests involved; stating the basis of findings — which will guarantee justice to the private interests. Many devices have been established, and as time goes on, they are being steadily refined. Thus the Rule of Law is established and maintained. The mistakes have been mistakes of inexperience; they are small compared with the mass of beneficent and authorized management of social affairs. There are always, in the interim, the check of the electoral process and of the Press, and the virile challenge of civic bodies.

The opposition — that is, the minority in the legislature — would be in the same position in a planned state as it is today, have the same rights of debate, the same rights of moving amendments, and of persuasion in committee and full assembly. Its power would still be derived from popular vote. There may always be a split in the majority itself, causing a change in its composition; and there may be cross-voting. Therefore what the electorate is likely to think of the behavior of the majority toward the minority will be a factor as important as it is in present circumstances. It must be assumed that only that series of statutes would be passed which a majority could persuade the voters to accept, and that the minority would have had rights of participating, as now, in the establishment of the laws. There is at present some agreement by the minority, or some of the minority, with what the majority does; and there have been instances where the majority itself has not been as solid an intellectual or emotional phalanx as Hayek insinuates from time to time.

Would any separate law be repealable if an election decided it should be? Of course it would. The electorate has been responsible for the establishment of the plan, its purposes, its instrumentalities, and its spirit and procedure. There is nothing whatever against its having second thoughts and changing its mind. It has done so from time to time already, by direct repeal; or there is a condoned neglect of enforcement and the law becomes a dead letter.

What is troublesome about the idea of repealing a law or a set of laws which govern production and distribution of wealth? That there is wasted expenditure, and that people who have been living under the expectation of one kind of law now must live under another. But that is part of freedom and progress; and the effect of disturbance will be weighed against the possible advantages of change. Even the rule of *stare decisis* is not allowed by educated judges to hold up essential change forever.

The people will do what they can bear and afford to do. All this implies that there will still be in full operation periodical elections and freedom of speech. Of course it does. That is the condition which in democracies will govern the pace and the comprehensiveness of their planning. Whatever proves itself satisfactory to the people, they having the untrammeled right to say what is and what is not unsatisfactory with all the vehemence which they like to use, will remain — even though there are as now, in every form of government, people who remain unpersuaded by the opinion of the majority. They may still inveigh against the law and its administration, and try to persuade the majority to adopt their views. No society has ever pretended that it is possible to operate with a unanimous vote, except the dictatorships. Should it happen that the only dissentient were Hayek, I am sure that, in a democracy, though he were thought to be obtuse or ill-informed or illogical, people would still listen to him and wonder.

Now it is manifest that time is of the essence of the consideration of the laws, for, as Bacon said, "Truth is the daughter of Time." Majority rule as it is, is admirably situated to compel caution to mingle with zeal, so that experiments are tried and the conditions of agreement and the combination of freedom with welfare discovered in the nationwide and study-small meeting of minds. If one postulates, quite unwarrantably, that a Plan is to appear full-fledged and abruptly, he has simply smuggled a fifth ace into the pack and produced it craftily. Those who play this trick must have the same reputation as card-players to whom the rules of the game mean no more.

It must be remembered that we are talking of this world outside the ivory tower of the web-spinning economist,

65

and particularly of the United States and Great Britain. Why Hayek postulates a group of planners estranged from, but dominating, the nation he does not say. It is a perfect obsession with him: ". . . an authority directing the whole economic system would be the most powerful monopolist conceivable . . . it would have complete power to decide what we are to be given and on what terms." (Page 93.) He doesn't say who would give "it" these monopolistic powers. "The power of the planner over our private lives does not depend on this [rationing and similar devices]. . . . The source of this power over all consumption which in a planned society the authority would possess would be its control over production." (Page 93.) Its source of power in actuality would not be this at all: it would be in the modulated, graduated authority responsibly conducted and regulated by the people. The difficulties of allocating rewards to competing groups he says "come to the surface only when a socialist policy is actually attempted with the support of the many different groups which together compose the majority of a people. Then it soon becomes the one burning question which of the different sets of ideals shall be *imposed upon all* by making the whole resources of the country serve it"! (Page 113. Italics mine.) Proof? The tactics of the Nazis in gaining power! (Pages 113-114.) The planner will coerce; the planner will need to create a myth; the planner will establish official doctrines; the planner only finds out about the conflicts between different needs as he goes along, and he has to make his decisions as the necessity arises. Then how did the planner get to be the planner? Who put him there? If he were *put* there, it implies that there were people who did this, and for a purpose; and that purpose, again, must have been formulated in law by the democratic and majority-minority processes we have described.

Why is this not discussed? It is simply to give the impression that a plan is an imposed thing, and not sprung from the vitals of the democratic people. Only if it is assumed that the planners impose themselves can Hayek arrive at the following conclusion: —

> What is called economic power, while it can be an instrument of coercion [he does not mean in economic individualism — perish the thought — but when used by the state] is, in the hands of private individuals, never exclusive or complete power, never power over the whole life of a person. But centralized as an instrument of political power it creates a degree of dependence scarcely distinguishable from slavery.[8]

Hayek's assumption is that political power is neither limited in scope, restricted in authority, responsible in operation, nor co-operative and decentralized in execution. This assumption is stupid.

[8] Hayek, *op. cit.*, pp. 145–146. Bracketed comment by present author.

CHAPTER V

# Adam Smith and Planning for Competition

> It was enough for them (who made the Constitution) to realize or to hope that they had created an organism; it has taken a century and has cost their successors much sweat and blood to prove that they created a nation. The case before us must be considered in the light of our whole experience and not merely in that of what was said a hundred years ago.
>
> — JUSTICE OLIVER WENDELL HOLMES
> in *Missouri* v. *Holland*

Adam Smith's *Wealth of Nations* was published in 1776. Not the first, or entirely original, it was the most comprehensive and penetrating treatise on economic wealth to his time. Hayek refers, and properly, with reverence to the master, but he has not made those adjustments on "the system of natural liberty" which Smith taught then, but beyond any doubt would have taught altogether differently if he now contemplated the prevalence of inequality and monopolies. Especially might we expect this since he was not only a master of economic theory, but of moral philosophy also.

Adam Smith taught that if men were left naturally free, that is without interference by government, in economic matters, their self-interest would lead them not only to contrive their own welfare, but necessarily that of the whole of society. Neither he nor practically any theorists or statesmen of his time rejected the paramount standard of national welfare or the propriety of government by the state. To the Fathers of the American Constitution, the powers delegated to the federal government, such as the regulation of commerce and immigration, included the power to plan.

Adam Smith did not use the term *laissez faire*. He borrowed the conception from his friends and teachers in France, the school known as the *économistes* or physiocrats, and accepted it as the basis of his work. These had a very special political task, to persuade away their government's minute regulation of industry, which had been in operation nearly three hundred years — which was limiting commerce within the country itself with import and export duties and prohibitions of manufacture and sale at home and abroad, with minute prescriptions of the quantity and quality of various goods to be manufactured, with antiquated systems of taxation, with theories for the retention of bullion in the country as the sinews of war, and so on. In England, especially affecting her trade with the American colonies and the West Indies, the situation was similar though not nearly so extreme. There were remnants of guild and corporate restrictions, and monopolies for the production of certain goods and trade with the colonies were put into the hands of certain companies. Agriculture in England was encouraged by export bounties and import restrictions. All this was a long, old growth. No survey had ever been made of the whole. Its administration was necessarily bad, since the science and traditions of good administration require long cultivation, or at least careful rational attention.

It was against this system that Adam Smith wrote, assuming that natural liberty would almost invariably produce a better result. *Laissez faire* meant "Let the government leave people to do what seems best to them." It did not mean the absence of all government: but it did not mean the presence of very much, at any rate to the French defenders. Adam Smith's principal protest was against the mercantile conception, that is, against restrictions on foreign trade; but he believed in the Navigation Act restrictions, as these strengthened national defense — or, as he said, "Defense comes before Opulence."

With his mind on ridding commerce of restrictions, he says, "Every individual is continually exerting himself to find out the most advantageous employment for whatever capital he can command. It is his own advantage, indeed, and not that of society, which he has in view. But the study of his own advantage naturally — or rather, necessarily — leads him to prefer that employment which is most advantageous to the society."[1] He then goes on to make a statement which has been the object of repeated quotation: —

As every individual, therefore, endeavours as much as he can both to employ his capital in the support of domestic industry, and so to direct that industry that its produce may be of the greatest value; every individual necessarily labours to render the annual value of the society as great as he can. He generally, indeed, neither intends to promote the public interest, nor knows how much he is promoting it. By preferring the support of domestic to that of foreign industry, he intends only his own security; and by directing that industry in such a manner as its produce may be of the greatest value, he intends only his own gain, and he is in this, as in many other cases, led by an invisible hand to promote an end which was no part of his intention.

[1] Adam Smith, *Wealth of Nations,* Bk. IV, Ch. 2.

Adam Smith has not said that this consonance of the individual gain with that of society is good for all fields of economic endeavor: it relates to the choice of preferring domestic to foreign trade, and then to "many other cases" — not *all* cases.

Then Smith after a short excursion says: "What is the species of domestic industry which his capital can employ, and of which the produce is likely to be of the greatest value, every individual it is evident, can, in his local situation, judge much better than any statesman or law-giver can do for him" — but this applies not to the contribution which the individual can make to the good of the society, or to any harm which the pursuit of his own interest might cause to other people, but only to the value which the user of the capital provides for himself.

Adam Smith is inveighing against the great merchants who had obtained monopolies on the excuse that it was good for the public, yet were in reality exploiting the wealth of the nation for their own benefit. It seems as though the tendency to monopoly were inherent in human nature: —

> To expect, indeed, that the freedom of trade should ever be entirely restored in Great Britain is as absurd as to expect that an Oceana or Utopia should ever be established in it. Not only the prejudices of the public, but what is much more unconquerable, the private interests of many individuals irresistibly oppose it.

Then he gives the warning which many Englishmen have given (but which is lost on Hayek, who teaches almost the reverse). Thus: —

> The violence and injustice of the rulers of mankind is an ancient evil for which I am afraid, the nature of human affairs can scarce admit of a remedy. But the mean rapacity, the monopolizing spirit of the merchants

and manufacturers, who neither are, nor ought to be, the rulers of mankind, though it cannot be corrected may very easily be prevented from disturbing the tranquility of anybody but themselves.[2]

Adam Smith assumes the existence of the laws of property, national defense, contract. He then adds some special duties: public works, the promotion and defense of foreign trade through arms and diplomacy, justice, and education. Here we intend only to consider education and public works.

Adam Smith advocates the imposition by the public on the "whole body of the people" of the necessity of acquiring the most essential parts of education, "by obliging every man to undergo an examination of probation in them before he can obtain the freedom in any corporation, or be allowed to set up trade either in a village or a town corporate."[3] But this is a strong intervention of the state: to be educated, at schools set up by the public, partly supported by it and partly by modest fees paid by the pupils, as a prerequisite to being able to earn one's living! They are to learn reading, writing and arithmetic, geometry and mechanics. There must be some serious necessity to support the government's compulsory action with so severe a sanction. The necessity is, indeed, of the gravest kind, in Adam Smith's opinion. He believes that where people are occupied day in, day out, with the subdivisions of a task in commercial society (and he was then speaking of the agricultural and small domestic crafts and very small workshops of his time) they become dull, apathetic, lose their spirit, especially their martial spirit, and become deficient in reasoning and judgment.

[2] *Op. cit.,* Bk. IV, Ch. 3.
[3] *Op. cit.,* Bk. V, Ch. 1.

The more they are instructed the less liable they are to the delusions of enthusiasm and superstition, which among ignorant nations, frequently occasion the most dreadful disorders. . . . An instructed and intelligent people . . . are more disposed to examine, and more capable of seeing through, the interested complaints of faction and sedition, and they are upon that account, less apt to be misled into any wanton or unnecessary opposition to the measures of the government. In free countries, where the safety of government depends very much upon the favourable judgment which the people may form of its conduct, it must surely be of the highest importance that they should not be disposed rashly or capriciously concerning it.

Hayek and his fellow serfs work themselves into a towering passion against socialists and planners, who, to support and get their government accepted and loyally operated, propose that the system of education should be conformable thereto. No system of government ever known has been able to dispense with an education appropriate to the objects of government. Note the wise Adam Smith. Note Aristotle; who, confronted with the problem of communism put before him by Plato, and unwilling to go as far as Plato, proposed not to equalize man's possessions, but rather to "equalize men's desires," by a "sufficient education provided by the state." Note that the French teachers of Adam Smith, whose motto was "Liberty and immunity are the best administrators, and government has practically nothing to do except to dispense itself from doing anything," were caught in their own logic: for the men who are economically anarchic must be wise to avoid damage to others. They could not be sure men would understand "the natural and essential order of political societies" which included their peculiar theory that only from the cultivation of the soil did wealth come. Education was, therefore, the first, essential, and sublime duty of the sovereign — free but compulsory. The task of our own day is the education of the integral democratic citizen. As Harrington said: "Education is the plastic art of government." Every state in history has used it; every family uses it; the capitalist state used it partly by withholding it; the democratic state in its search for the way out of the deficiencies of economic individualism will give it to itself.

On the question of the positive action of the state, Adam Smith has a wise maxim: —

> The third and last duty of the sovereign or commonwealth is that of erecting and maintaining those public institutions and those public works, which though they may be in the highest degree advantageous to a great society are, however, of such a nature that the profit could never repay the expense to any individual or small number of individuals, and which it cannot therefore be expected that any individual or small number of individuals should erect or maintain. The performance of this duty requires, too, very different degrees of expense in the different periods of society.

Adam Smith refers to good roads, bridges, navigable canals, harbors, and the like — and generally to the "erection and maintenance of the public works which facilitate the commerce of any country." "Commerce" then meant all economic activities other than subsistence agriculture. There are no reservations on whether or not there should be positive governmental promotion of business, or undertaking of activities by government itself.

Naturally, we can think of works which the advance of technical knowledge put entirely beyond Smith's ken: —

1. The conservation of natural resources, protectively and directively, and directly conducted if necessary by Government.

2. Government exploitation.

   (*a*) Where the economic returns are indirect for all society, and (where the investment is very long term and) the monetary profit does not come at all or altogether from the particular works — thus, for example, the grant of credit, exploiting hydroelectric power; planting a dust-bowl area, or clearing a cut-over region, or establishing storehouses, refrigeration, and processing plants;

   (*b*) Where the capital required is so great, if the economy of the exploitation is to be at its best, that as in the case of Boulder Dam (or say the establishment of a steel or cement industry or the hydrogenation of coal), it is unlikely to be accumulated in the lifetime of those who conceive the project, yet needs backing to get started;

   (*c*) Where works of pivotal importance and lease of natural resources are involved (for example, in the case of fuel, power, communications, or a chemical industry);

   (*d*) Great basic public needs — health, the feeding and clothing of children, housing, varying with time — which private business cannot supply properly because the inequality of fortunes causes other less important wants to be taken care of first;

   (*e*) Schemes of development where a number of industrial, agricultural, and commercial considerations must be integrated, for the best economy of the system, and where the appropriate combination of technical skill, ideas, public incentive, and sovereign power over persons and property are required for success, yet could not be conceded to private persons, as the power would be too great. For example, the T.V.A., or the plans of economic development for India or China, or the work done by the Chilean Development Corporation.

All this is in addition to a concern for the direction of investment and of the "labor market," direction of the location of industry if it should happen otherwise to be against the public interest, the social services of health, nutrition, housing, and social insurance, which offer a wide and clear field of planning by federal, state, and local government. In addition to these, we could mention that now there is the enforcement of competition and fair business where otherwise there would be monopoly, force, and fraud.

Hayek agrees that where it is impracticable to make the enjoyment of certain services dependent on the payment of a price (as with signposts in the roads, and "in most circumstances . . . the roads themselves") the state should undertake the works; that the state should also take action where there is a divergence between the items which enter into private calculation and those which affect social welfare — and as when the damage caused to others by certain uses of property cannot properly be charged to the owner of the property (as, deforestation, some methods of farming, or the smoke and noise of factories). He concedes that there ought to be factory and building regulations (Page 81) and prevention of fraud, of deception and of the exploitation of ignorance in industry. He agrees to the building of dams (but as far as I can make out not to the production of electricity, or to the making of massive machinery). He seems responsive to the claims of social insurance, on the grounds that there are some risks which are intolerable (but he is not specific about this, nor is he prepared for a compulsory arrangement).[4]

Hayek requires one thing more of the state, and it is his chief positive action: he requires that the state shall act to make competition as "effective as possible." It is to provide a framework which will make competition work — that is, it is to break down all rigidities. "The question whether the state should or should not 'act' or 'interfere' poses an altogether false alternative, and the term 'laissez faire' is a highly ambiguous and misleading description of the principles on which a liberal policy is based." (Pages 80–81.) We must choose, he thinks, between competition or complete regulation, for it is impossible to combine competition with planning to any extent we like without the combination ceasing to operate as an effective guide to production: "Both competition and central direction become poor and inefficient tools if they are incomplete; they are alternative principles used to solve the same problem, and a mixture of the two means that neither will really work and that the result will be worse than if either system had been consistently relied upon." (Page 42.) (Let it be noted before we proceed that this is false reasoning: the value of the result depends upon the ends to be sought in the planning, where there is an organized system.)

Hayek goes on: "It is of the utmost importance to the argument of this book for the reader to keep in mind that the planning against which all our criticism is directed is solely the planning against competition — the planning

[4] This appears from a printed summary of a Radio Forum of the University of Chicago, April 22, 1945, p. 4.

which is to be substituted for competition." He then abdicates a responsibility in a most disconcerting manner: he finds he will not have time in the book to say what the planning *for* competition shall be, in spite of the fact that if it were sound it would be the best positive argument he could adduce in support of his case!

We must supply what Hayek omits. It must be remembered that the preservation of competition is to be entrusted to the coercive power of the government. This must be incessant. It could not be done once and for all, because the tendencies *against* competition are inherent, and will up again as soon as suppressed.

These, then, are the minimum activities the government would have to undertake to enforce free competition: —

1. Disperse all monopolies.
2. Equalize fortunes.
3. Annihilate coercion, fraud, and favoritism in business practice.
4. Equalize Education.
5. Indoctrinate Education and use Propaganda.
6. Liquidate trade-unions and political parties who preach planning.
7. Establish an unamendable constitution; or an oligarchic one limiting the majority and the legislature.

1. *The dispersion of monopolies* would require a law defining monopoly, stating penalties, and setting up an agency to administer it — that is, it would require civil servants, otherwise known by the fearful designation "bureaucrats." The bureaucrats would have to distinguish between the rights of combination for the purpose of better use of modern technology and large-scale economies, and collusion against public policy. This would require a great staff, and many inquiries, and interference with businessmen, the production of documents and sworn statements, and even the

use of plain-clothes detectives and spies to see that the officials of the businesses were speaking the truth, for they have been known to equivocate and act dumb. Lie detectors ought to be used, for if we are properly to enforce competition, we must not be unjust to anybody who might like to try to enter the business with a special genius for reducing costs, yet he might be kept out by negligence on the part of the public authority in not discovering all his obstructors. A school would need to be set up for the inspectorial and detective staff, so that they could learn the tricks of "gentlemen's agreements," secret rebates, and the sharing of the market and profits, and other such attempts at collusion. It might be useful to connect all the potential monopolists to the central authority with portable radios, on the principle that the earliest intimation of intention to combine or evade the law is the best way of dealing with the powerful.

In addition, it would be proper to prescribe enforcement of orders to disperse. This might be done by heavy taxation, with the risk of its evasion. Criminal sentences would be necessary, as also outlawry with penalties and damages awardable to all those injured by collusive action, and physical intervention against the various officials and their plant and offices. As action against the monopolies in the United States has hitherto not had a very striking result, it would be necessary to increase considerably the staff of the Federal Trade Commission and the Department of Justice, and the number of attorneys concerned with prosecutions.

It would also be essential to abolish any tariff duties that have the effect of assuring the interests a market, which are an inducement to combine to secure it. This would involve the attendant changes in the various branches of industry and agriculture which have reached a certain integration and price structure by the aid of tariffs.

If the monopolies were dispersed, there would still be the problem of restoring responsible control to business corporations, with the real stimulus of economic individualism behind it. There would need to be established a government department to investigate the actual controls and the relationships of ownership to direction and management of the firms. The owners would be forced to surrender their holdings to the directors and management, who would pay for the stock with money provided by government loans, or the owners could be forced to attend the shareholders' meetings. As attendance at the meetings would be useless without knowledge enough to control policy, and thus be good competitors with other firms and keep their directors up to the mark, owners of stock would have to be compelled to read the reports and to repair to government schools, where, as Adam Smith proposed, they would learn reading, writing, accounting, geometry and mechanics, before they were further admitted to the trade they wished to pursue. They must be forced to do it. Forced to be free! The bliss!

To get competition among firms with large capital — how is that possible? Only by setting up competitors who have interesting ideas and good projects and yet may not accumulate the necessary capital before they die. This means that to maintain competition the government planner for free-for-all competition must provide or guarantee credit to would-be competitors. To anybody? If he does not take anybody but chooses his particular people, it would set up a rising howl throughout the land; while if he did not choose among them, there would be a great many failures, and charlatans would run the government into bad debts. If he selected the creditors, by what criterion would he choose? It would have to be a guess that they were good competitive material in some particular line of business. And here Hayek's own planner would have to make *distinctions between persons for particular objects* — which he said was against natural law. It is to such absurdity that the insensate attachment to unmitigated bigotry is bound to lead.

As a matter of fact, the Reconstruction Finance Corporation does provide such credits and a study of the Corporation would show Hayek that (*a*) he cannot lend to everybody because it is the nation's money that is being ventured, and (*b*) it is difficult to control the situation unless the government — and government-trusted appointed officials — run the mines, drill for oil, conduct the factories, develop the estates. For then the guess as to the creditability and efficiency of the private entrepreneur is supplanted by full authority to choose the man and the right to control him afterwards. In the existing situation, the R.F.C. either gets its money back or it does not; and the reason so much of the money is repaid is that the R.F.C. does not take all the risks it might. Would it be permissible for an applicant to go to the ordinary courts of the land and argue that the discretion vested in H.R.F.C.F.C. (Hayek's Reconstruction Finance Corporation for Competition) was in conflict with Hayek's bill of rights to the effect that "No man shall be deprived of state credit, that is to say, of competitive opportunity, without due process of law"? If this were not permitted, what assurance would there be that the H.R.F.C.F.C. were not playing favorites? How could you be sure, where the intensity of competition was so encouraged, that the Hayekian Commissioners would not take bribes? Police upon police! Let us recall how astounded were congressmen at the discovery of the discretion they themselves had accorded to the administrator, and then how they refused to have Henry Wallace when they had lost Jesse Jones. Personal custodianship enters again: not the "blind forces" of competition.

It cannot be done — not 100 per cent; and if not 100 per cent, the distinction between planning *for* competition and planning *against* competition for the common welfare is blurred.

2. *It would be necessary to equalize fortunes* to make

sure that competitive equality prevailed. It would not be useless when we were doing this to compensate as well by a little extra aid those who had some personal blemish which detracted from their chances to compete along the lines where their ability was specifically better than that of other people. (John Stuart Mill, incidentally, proposes this.) Thus a very good salesman with a persuasive voice, and argumentative and impressive powers, yet so short as to be ridiculous, might be provided with special boots; or, put at a disadvantage by nature with a face uglier than his "approach," might receive plastic surgery or a mask. But apart from these cases, which would involve much personal discrimination, it would be most seriously necessary to give the rein to ability to satisfy the market by reducing the obstacles of inequality of fortunes. What an inquisition this would require! What searches! What hunting for definitions!

From the standpoint of such competition alone, the surest way to start people off equally, as regards fortune, is to abolish all property for productive purposes that is in private hands. If it is really intended to make competition work, this is the way to do it. Its eugenic effect was long ago recommended by Bernard Shaw. The Soviet system has adopted this principle, for the very reason now being discussed: to cast off the trammels of inequality on production and happiness. I think this is excessive: but it is the logical consequence of absolute attachment to a single principle of economic organization that in Hayek's case is competition.

He must see to it that the children in the various families are not only not allowed to enter into an inheritance at the death of their parents which would disturb the equality of a starting opportunity to compete, but also that while children they are prevented from receiving better food and better treatment, which are bound to increase their competitive efficiency and thus give them extra rewards for less effort.

For the belief in the beneficence of competition is an important foundation of its continuance; and it will not be believed in, if some seem to get a better chance. Three consequences would seem to follow: that parents should be paid equally, whatever their competitive ability; that children of the poor should be subsidized by allowances from the public purse; that the children should all be sent to schools maintained by the public, where their treatment would be entirely equal.[5]

It should be observed, further, that what has been said on the subject of the equalization of fortunes in all its aspects could not be implemented merely by statute, but would need a great investigatory staff and enforcement officers, especially to see that secret bribes and commissions were not given to subvert the intentions of law.[6]

3. *The annihilation of force, fraud, and favoritism in the general practice of trade.* This raises at least all the problems that have been raised by the stultified work of the Federal Trade Commission, the Department of Justice, and the codes under the NRA. Think of the millions of transactions that occur in all branches of economic activity every day! Where is the state administration of Hayek going to begin and end? The Hayekian administration will not know at the outset where the rot that cripples and falsifies competition may begin: the misnaming of goods, unfair preference of one customer to another, corrupt statement of ingredients or performance, additional deliveries as gifts, surly and deterrent service, misrepresentation of competi-

[5] Adam Smith, *Wealth of Nations,* Bk. V, Ch. 1. Let us remember one admonition of Adam Smith's: that civil government is established by property owners to safeguard their property; and that property and birth give those who benefit from both the major sway in the operation of government.

[6] John Locke's way of avoiding these troubles will be remembered: that no one should have more property than he could put his own labor into, for his own immediate consumption.

tor's goods. Hayek has said that any encroachment on competition runs through the whole apparatus and prevents other people from planning their competition as they wish to do. This holds good of coercion and fraud and intrigue used by private persons, not officials, in competitive trade. Millions of transactions means that there are millions of loopholes and that misdemeanors will occur unless the state puts its fingers on all. It is a well-known principle of police administration that if possible the state should act preventively and not merely punitively; that the network of agents should be spread as broadly as the potential malefactors. This is a great task to which Hayek has set his hand, since it would imply that the books and records of all traders should be available for periodical inspection, and that such inspection should take much time.

4. *Education must be equalized.* All need not be taught the same things, but all must have the opportunity they want to develop those talents they think can be best used in the market. The state would need to attend to this much more thoroughly than it does today anywhere in the world, and to exclude unequalizing private lessons.

5. *But the object of education would not merely be training for occupations and professions; there must necessarily be tutoring in the theory of the competitive state.* It must be demonstrated that this is the desirable state of man; and, indeed, a propaganda ought really to be carried on, from the earliest time that the child can consciously absorb the meaning of the lessons applied in a suitable technical way, teaching the beneficence of the system of Hayek. For nearly all men and women have troubles of conscience and anxieties about the worth and destiny of humanity. It could not be expected that they all innately think alike about the system of competition. There may be some, like Robert Owen or Edward Bellamy, who do not think it proper to beat down and cast out other human beings; or who think

84

it wrong to work at the things and at the pace which the rest of mankind forces on them since the power of the majority is determining the choices of the minority. Or there may be men like John Stuart Mill who begin to think, in middle life, that the way of social happiness lies in socialism.[7] There are people of this kind, we know. For there are socialist and co-operative producers, and co-operative consumers' movements. What is to be done about these, by a state which plans only *for* competition? Is there to be a Sedition Law making it an offense to speak publicly with the effect of seducing others from observance of the principles of Hayek's bill of rights, with intent to subvert the constitution of economic individualists?

The problem here is that the system of economic enterprise, its methods and its spirit, are inseparable from the rest of the human personality. What is to be done about those who hear voices about monetary theory, about justice, about security? Indoctrinate for competition, or risk its subversion?

6. *The trade-unions would be abolished* as collective bargaining agents, or as the users of power against the power of property. The methods that could be followed in this respect are so well known to students of labor history — Pinkerton detectives, tear-gas bombs, seizure of funds, prohibitions of association, yellow-dog contracts, refusals to recognize, victimization — that it is not necessary to detail this further.

It would be necessary to prohibit political parties that were hostile to planning, as their literature, meetings, and speeches would be directed to undermining the principle of planning for competition. They might even lead to a tax strike against agencies that were especially critical in their operation, and they would be worrying to the government and departments who were elected to administer the statutes.

[7] *Cf.* p. 29 above.

7. *Finally, the Constitution would be unamendable.* As the opposition, if it were allowed to exist, might persuade people against the system of economic individualism *in gloriam,* its opposition would have to be curbed. This could only be done by enshrining the bill of rights of Hayek, that is, economic individualism, in the Constitution, and then making the Constitution unamendable.

There is but one outlet for the dissatisfied under an unamendable constitution, known to all theories of tyranny. It is revolution. This is the logical consequence of *The Road to Serfdom.*

# CHAPTER VI

# "Dictatorship" Means Dictatorship

> The surest way to prevent seditions (if the times do bear it) is to take away the matter of them.
>
> — FRANCIS BACON

Hayek pretends that the "socialist" ideas he heard twenty or twenty-five years ago in Austria and Germany were responsible for dictatorship in those countries! Having lived in those countries, and now living in England and observing America, he wants us to believe he is abler at appreciating this relationship of ideas to events.

> Thus, by moving from one country to another, one may sometimes twice watch similar phases of intellectual development. The senses have then become peculiarly acute. When one hears for a second time opinions expressed or measures advocated which one has first met twenty or twenty-five years ago, they assume a new meaning as symptoms of a definite trend. . . . It is necessary now to state the unpalatable truth that it is Germany whose fate we are in some danger of repeating.[1]

There is a half-hearted admission on the same page (but then left to rot there without influence on his subsequent

---

[1] Hayek, *The Road to Serfdom*, p. 2.

declaration of reactionary terror) that "conditions in England and the United States are still so remote from those witnessed in recent years in Germany as to make it difficult to believe that we are moving in the same direction." But those conditions have been different from the beginning of time, and the Germans have been in Germany from the beginning of recorded time. Their mind has been vastly different always, their conditions such as to produce an almost unbroken dictatorial government from the early sixteenth century down to our own days. How wrong, indeed how iniquitous, it is to argue that there is the *same* determination in the three countries to retain the organization for defense for purposes of "creation"! How mischievous and unscientific, how anti-intellectual, to assert that there is the *same* "spurious realism" and even cynicism; the *same* fatalistic acceptance of "inevitable trend."

He must pin upon socialism the production of Fascism and Nazism. This perversion is thus expressed: —

> Few are ready to recognize that the rise of fascism and naziism was not a reaction against the socialist trends of the preceding period but a necessary outcome of those tendencies. This is a truth which most people were unwilling to see even when the similarities of many of the repellent features of the internal regimes in communist Russia and National Socialist Germany were widely recognized.

Fascism and Nazism did not arise out of socialism. Only if we exclude from socialism its generous and equalizing humanitarian purpose, its democratic evolution, its solicitude and kindness to men and women, its profound sense of justice, its love of literature and the arts, its celebration of

[2] *Op. cit.,* pp. 3–4.

family joys, and if, especially concentrating on British socialism, we exclude from it the impulses and restraints of its Christian origins and fostering — if, in short, we exclude all ends and all spirit — we might, by some stretch of a nightmare, think as Hayek talks.

Fascists and Nazis were certainly in revolt against the capitalist order; but they hated the socialists of their countries: they imprisoned, exiled, or killed them. The Nazis and Fascists were voted against, while voting was still possible, by socialists. Moreover, politics were different in the two countries. In Italy, the Fascist regime was set up chiefly by the violent and personal ambitions of Mussolini. Had there been no Mussolini, there would have been no Fascism. But there might have been the institution of a democratic socialist government, by parliamentary methods, if we may judge from the steady advance of socialist voting strength in municipal government. In the Italian parliament the Socialist Party reached its maximum representation in November 1919, with almost 30 per cent of the seats; at the time of the March on Rome, October 1922, it held only about 20 per cent of the seats in the Chamber of Deputies. Even then it is doubtful whether a Socialist Party government would have been possible without the advent of coalition governments including other parties and especially the very large, Catholic Popular Party. These inclusions would have meant a very, very gradual development of the social services rather than the socialization of the means of production or the nationalization of the land. It would possibly have meant the disintegration of the great estates, the *latifundia,* and so the creation of small private enterprise in agriculture, perhaps benefiting from modern agricultural technology as the result of government-fostered cooperatives.

Does Hayek rely on the fact that Mussolini himself was formerly a "socialist"? He called himself a "socialist" — but look at his record.[8] Mussolini was revolutionary and dictatorial by character, and it was open to him to take advantage of or to be generous with the torments of Italy resulting from World War I. Her material losses, the desertions of her soldiers disaffected because they did not believe in the war, the profiteering as the result of the war, the hopes of improved economic constitutions kindled by the leaders, the determination of certain young adventurers of all parties not to come back to the peaceful life where everything has its place, where there is social discipline, and where business and the professions demand industry and patience but do not grant the authority over other people and the prestige and distinction that many had had in the armed forces. All these things are well known except to Hayek.

There was unemployment. There were high prices and scarcity. The war had been entered into for gain — sacred egoism. Italy was almost new to democracy. The people were largely illiterate. Industrialization was recent and petty. The parliamentary system had been corrupt; it had not given equality of opportunity; the workers' movement had been bitterly repressed with the force of arms again and again, even for singing their own hymns; the anarchic syndicalist movement rather than the democratic parliamentary gradualist school of socialist thought had attracted many Italian workers.

Yet the great mass of the Socialist Party, almost to a man, detested and despised Mussolini. Indeed, they expelled him in November 1914, because he was corrupt, ruthless, and lacking in the democratic temperament. There was only one way available to him to return to politics in 1919, and that was by fomenting trouble, by stirring up international and domestic violence, in the factories, on the land and in the

[8] It is written amply in my *Mussolini's Italy,* the first work to portray the inward weakness and sham nature of the dictatorship. Also *cf.* Salvemini, *Under the Axe of Fascism.*

streets, in order to draw attention to himself and get the leadership of the party victorious in that violence. The victors were the middle and upper classes, in a panic at the idea of social unrest and the possible advance of socialist movement: in a panic, not because the socialist program or tactics or real chances of getting a majority in a short time justified a panic — but in rather the same sort of panic as Hayek exhibits at the present moment. And so the discard of the Socialist Party, never a democrat, led the panic-stricken middle and upper classes into power in 1922, and in the course of a few years scattered, murdered, or exiled the members of the Socialist Party.

This is the true, well-authenticated history of the rise of Italian Fascism. It was not that the socialists were too hard, or too planful, or too resolute. They were not ruthless when others flew to the sword instead of the ballot boxes. By pretending that Italian Fascism was the natural extension and the actual carrying out of the socialist movement, Hayek is able to attribute the horrors of Fascism to the socialist idea and program. And then he recounts Fascism's methods, as we have had them described to us again and again, especially since World War II has overthrown certain suspicious inhibitions and enabled the true, despicable features of the regime to be published, instead of complacent stories that the trains were on time in Fascist Italy. What was atrocious about this Fascist regime was not, as Hayek wishes us to believe, the inherent result of its planning — for it did not plan, except for war. It was the direct result of the inherent spirit of its makers. It was the reign of a brutal, callous, cynical dictator and his gang, around whom rallied, not the workers but the middle and upper class; even then, not all of those were serious — they had merely forgotten their responsibilities as citizens of a democracy long enough for the toughs and racketeers to win. All that came of the regime was the product of the dictatorial spirit of its deliberate creators. In fact, with the exception of some social services partly designed as a sop to the workers and partly as means to increase the population and fitness of the people for war, the system of capitalism went on satisfactorily — except that those most subject to its oppression were the workers, who were not even allowed to have their own independent trade-unions, which make up the only force they can use against the massive power of inert property. There were many people in Great Britain and the United States and France who praised this regime; but they were not socialists, or liberals — they were the same kind of men as those who now applaud *The Road to Serfdom*.

Turn now to Germany and the Nazis. Again, it is Hayek's thesis that the socialists prepared the way, were the cause of Germany's descent into Nazism. He argues his points in the following stages. Since 1870 the Social Democratic Party had taught people to hate the profit motive, and espoused the growth of cartels and combines and monopolies on technological grounds for efficiency's sake; it split the country by adherence to the Marxist faith, thus bringing about social hatred; and it organized the party with children's organizations and the teaching of a generally socialist way of life which comprehended all aspects of man's existence. Moreover the Social Democrats, he says, engaged in many schemes, leading to the planning of the nation when the system of private enterprise was abolished. They were leading exponents of planning.

This, like his description of Italian Fascism, is the most unhistorical nonsense imaginable. Germany never knew what democracy was until 1919, when a republican constitution, the Weimar Constitution, modeled roughly on those of France, Great Britain and the United States, was set up. There never was in Germany until 1919 a freely elected *responsible* sovereign government. Till then, the government was in the hands of the hereditary ruler of

Prussia, the descendant of the Hohenzollern family. The system was a monarchy, though it was so late in the day in the development of political forms. But it was limited by the collaboration of the legislature, the Reichstag, elected every four years by universal male suffrage. The industrial areas were gerrymandered out of their due representation, which would have meant a substantial power for the working-class representatives — that is, to a Social Democratic Party. Government was, therefore, in the hands of the monarch, his ministerial representatives, and the representatives of the nonworking-class groups. Between 1878 and 1890, Bismarck conducted a bitter mass persecution and banning of the Socialist Party (which had twelve seats in the Reichstag!) in the hope of destroying what he called "a troop of bandits." In Prussia, which was two thirds of Germany, matters were even worse: for there the parliament had even less power.[4] It was elected by a three-class system whereby the few people who paid the top third of the tax roll had one third of the votes; the next class (larger, of course) also received a third of the votes; and the tremendous number of the poor followed. Thus — in 1913 — a voter in the first tax class had four times the representative power of one in the second and over sixteen times that of one in the third class. Here was property insuring itself with a vengeance — a most interesting extension of the system of economic individualism.

The German Reich, in short, was made by this constitution thoroughly safe for economic individualism — for all, that is, except the vast majority, who were without the capital to take advantage of it.

As for having a *Weltanschauung,* that is a world conception of a wide sociological and philosophical nature, everybody in Germany — the land of political romanticism —

[4] There had never been a parliament at all until 1852, though the English had had one since 1295.

had, and has, an opinionated world outlook. That is the trouble. The Germans are not skeptics, cool and moderate, as the English and the Americans are. They are not easy, nor afflicted with the illness which Hayek calls the "malady of the muddled middle." They are philosophical people, and they take their philosophy as seriously as though all their surmises were true. They carry through to a logical conclusion in terms of behavior those occasional flashes of illumination we all have, and believe their logical structures to be uncompromising orders to act. That is where Nazism springs from, not from the socialists. The Germans have had more philosophers than any other single country, and they have almost always had harsher dictatorial government than anywhere else. Yes — as Goethe, who had much experience in administration, complained of them in the *Conversations* with Eckermann (March 12, 1828): "They are entirely absorbed in the Idea, and only the highest problems of speculation are fitted to interest them. . . . If we could only alter the Germans after the model of the English, less theory and more practice, we might obtain a good share of redemption."

Compare a list of characteristic British writers on public affairs with a list of German. The former would contain Hobbes, Locke, Harrington, Hume, Burke, Adam Smith, Bentham, the Mills, Herbert Spencer, T. H. Green; the latter, Kant, Hegel, Fichte, Gentz, Adam Müller, Humboldt, Schopenhauer, Nietzsche, Marx, and Spengler. It is no accident that societies which so consistently produce such contrasting types are separated as widely in the spirit, the purposes, and the institutions of their government.

Heine, who because he fought in the cause of Freedom was forced to flee from Germany after writing some of its loveliest poetry and songs, said of the differing conceptions of liberty in France, Britain, and Germany: —

As for the Germans, they need neither freedom nor equality. They are a speculative race, ideologists, prophets and reflective dreamers who only live in the past and the future, and have no present. Englishmen and Frenchmen have a *present* — with them, every day has its field of action, its opposing element, its history. . . . It cannot be denied that the Germans love liberty: but it is in a different fashion than other people. The Englishman loves liberty as his lawful wife, and if he does not treat her with any special tenderness, he is still ready whenever necessary to defend her like a man, and woe to the soldier who forces his way to her bedroom. . . . The Frenchman loves liberty as his bride. He burns for her, he is aflame, he casts himself at her feet with the most prodigal protestations, he will fight for her to the death, and commit for her sake a thousand follies. The German loves liberty as though she were his old grandmother.

The Germans lost a constitution in 1848, because they philosophized while the king's soldiers fired. Between 1925 and 1933 they argued away their liberties by philosophies. The attitude of the man who says, "I'm from Missouri" is a very important instrument of democracy: and it is heard, thank heavens, throughout the length and breadth of the United States.

Germany has never known the liberty that comes when a land makes a revolution and either executes a king, as in England, or does away with kingship as in the United States. Germany (or rather the Germanic state) was almost always a "planned" state, because the kings and the upper classes never let the economy really get out of their hands from the time in the sixteenth century when the chief domains were the king's property. The peasants were serfs until 1811. The German states were the great practitioners of cameralism, the policy and practice of state economy. Prussia was a nation which had a bureaucracy properly trained and schooled two hundred years before Great Britain and the United States. The nation was militaristic through and through, for reasons of geography and of psychology. Its economy and society were militaristic — and had nothing to do with socialism. The army gradually assumed almost entire direction of the economy; because this first standing army in Europe needed wealth, the king wanted to have wealth. The historian Ernst von Meier, whose authority Hayek can hardly disavow, states that by the beginning of the eighteenth century, *"Prussia was then not a land with an army, but an army with a land."* And this gave Prussia and various of the other Germanic states — and the Reich of 1867 and 1871 made by "blood and iron" in war, and by Prussian military and economic coercion, and then dominated by Prussia — the character which it was never able to shake off: orders from above, obedience from below. Or, as the Nazi jurists phrased it, responsibility upwards, and authority from above downwards! This is what the socialists wanted to overturn; not to use. The Social Democratic Party was the stoutest opponent of the Nazis and of the German Communists, opposing both of them because they were totalitarian and nondemocratic.

When therefore the unhistorical Hayek, who attempts to rest his case on the pickings of history, says "Let us begin at 1870," he is two hundred and fifty years too late. When the great new industry sprang up in Germany (she was almost altogether agricultural and small commerce and handicrafts to 1870), of course it would be through modern methods, namely, organized combines; of course it would use the most advanced technology; of course it would be at the time of the reaction from *laissez faire* in other countries (*Munn* v. *Illinois* was decided in the United States Supreme

Court in 1871); and of course it therefore would be with state connivance and state assistance and participation, because there was the ulterior purpose of national strength for intervention in world affairs with predatory intent.

What a different course of history from that of America and Great Britain! The proof that the two peoples are different lies in their institutions and their history. Their institutions have made their history, which is the character of a people in operation.

Hitler was not a socialist. He was a nationalist and a racialist; and in *Mein Kampf* himself tells how he designed to use social services and equality for the purpose of the Reich for conquest of the world. The purposes of socialism —equality, prosperity, charity, and international peace— were not the aims of Hitler. He detested all of them. It is irrelevant altogether to quote to us, as Hayek does, a number of obscure economic professors who may have impressed him when he was a student, men who said they were socialists but who characteristically derided Great Britain because she was a nation of merchants, while Germany was a nation of heroes! The writings he refers to were written in the course of World War I and were war polemics.

The German General Staff, who had expected to win World War I in a rush, found themselves by the end of 1915 faced with a task they had not expected. They needed total mobilization of everything for the single purpose of winning the war, and war is a pre-emptory master. There arose the term *Planwirtschaft,* a planned economy, on the foundations of *Wehrwirtschaft,* a military economy. It was not far to go then to change *Planwirtschaft* into *Gemeinwirtschaft,* a communal economy, or an economy directed to the attainment of the maximum common welfare. But socialists in democratic Germany preferred to proceed by compromise and commissions for the study of feasible socialization, not to clap a plan on the German people. The militarists, however, when the war came to an end, did not stop their thinking. Ludendorff, the commander in chief who had ordered total mobilization of German industry and man power and agriculture, now produced a book with the title of *Der Totale Krieg;* [5] he was the first totalitarian.

As war is the highest tension of a people for self-preservation, so Total Politics in peacetime must be the preparation for this national struggle in war and must consolidate the foundations for the struggle in such strength, so that no severity of war, or measures of the enemy can make headway against these foundations or completely destroy them. . . . In the economic sphere fighting forces and people constitute a mighty unity. Total Politics and Total War Leadership cannot learn this too soon in peacetime.

The Racial Soul, the Blood and Soil of the Fatherland, must be pervaded with the sense of the mission of war. To this end Christianity must be subverted, and the best model to take is "the solidarity of the Japanese people," the Shinto faith. There must be complete industrial organization always for the one end. Ludendorff is available for Hayek and his zealots to read. Hitler read him and carried on to the logical conclusion.[6] It must never be forgotten that for the German people, with the exception of some millions of Social Democrats, World War I did not end in 1918.

Can we take the points of the Nazi program of 1920 seriously? The Nazis did not; most "socialists" with Hitler left him in 1927, and others were massacred by him (June

[5] Translated 1936 as *The Nation at War* (London).
[6] Ludendorff was Hitler's companion in the Munich plot of 1923, but refused to have anything more to do with him after Hitler's exhibition of cowardice under fire.

1934) — if those ruffians can be called "socialists." At any rate half of those points were anti-Semitic; the others were a mixed selection of proposals of extended social services, control over trusts and the like, support of the middle class; in an "explanation," it was observed that the Nazi Party stood for the principle of private property. Hitler did not make his way to office by such promises. He made his way to office chiefly by activating the spirit of military revenge for the defeat of Germany in the last war, and on top of this by promising every group whatever it wanted to meet its troubles. He won power by exploiting the desire to wipe out the humiliation of a defeat and of the subsequent treaty — which, just as it was and even generous, could hardly be regarded by a conquered people as other than unjust and shameful.

The new democratic system could not stand against such tactics. It was made the butt of the lost war and the fulfillment of the peace terms. The militarists, the Nationalist Party, the conservative groups, the *Junkers,* and the big industrialists supported Hitler in the first instance. Dr. H. E. Fried has, in his *Guilt of the German Army,* told with unrelenting veracity the story of the guilt of the German army and their friends in establishing Hitler. Professor Konrad Heiden, in his history of the Nazi Party and in *Der Führer,* has confirmed this, and told how the industrialists and big financiers financed Hitler. And Herr Thyssen, who wanted a restoration of monarchy, has added a personal touch to the story: —

After 1930 the aspirations of German industry may be summed up in one phrase: "A sound economy in a strong state." This was, I remember, the slogan of a meeting of the Ruhr industrialists in 1931. . . . But I also believed that by backing Hitler and his party I could contribute to the reinstatement of real government and of orderly conditions, which would enable all branches of activity — and especially business — to function normally once again. But it is no use crying over spilt milk! [7]

Could anything be more innocent to an economic individualist? These men did not want socialism, nor did they want the planned state, though they may have wanted the *fixed* state, fixed for themselves as rulers, in the name of economic individualism. Indeed, Hayek would seem to be in bad company, for this is how the worst got to the top.

Added to these factors were the young people, born a little before the war, who knew no tranquil regime, but were thrown into the great postwar fevers of the Continent in a direly defeated country. It was the young who could be most made to feel the shame of a war they had never fought in, and they voted for Hitler. Furthermore, the middle classes, ruined by the deliberate inflation of the mark, and impoverished by the war and by reparations payments (not much of the latter), felt the most serious uncertainty and insecurity, and above all a malicious resentment against the working classes — who were better organized, did basic work, and seemed to threaten the social position of the white-collared worker. Millions suffered from the mass unemployment which started in late 1928. This helped to swell the Hitler vote, although it never reached a majority. Those who voted for him voted not for a planned state, but for military strength, hope, and work, an exit from anxieties. They did not know that his purposes were otherwise, and were too miserable or too ignorant or too ruthless to care.

All the long and sadistic account of the actions of Hitler's regime — how it formulated a doctrine, set up a single

[7] Fritz Thyssen, *I Paid Hitler,* p. 32.

monopolistic political party (Hayek does not enter into the problem of the Dictatorial Party which is the essence of totalitarianism), tried to foist a new morality on the people, established secret police, imprisoned opposition leaders, corrupted the schools and textbooks, and executed those who did not submit to *The Plan* — is true but irrelevant. It was necessary for Douglas Miller to write that remarkably intelligent book, *You Can't Do Business with Hitler*, as an antidote to the economic individualists who believed business possible and profitable.[8] No democratic party or party leader, and hardly an independent private thinker, has ever proposed or countenanced such a system of government. Dictatorship lies in the spirit of the regime, for this has produced its advent, its triumph, and its machinery. First is will; systems are derivative.

On grounds of history; on grounds of logic; on grounds of the misuse of terms; of the abuse of authorities; of the neglect of verified information; of the use of the most infantile fallacy known to logic, viz. *post hoc, ergo propter hoc* — Hayek's attempt to identify socialism and planning and dictatorship and totalitarianism is not only a failure, it is a snare.

This leaves us with Russia, about which, curiously, Hayek says very little. Is Russia a case of socialist planning, and therefore dictatorship? Russia is socialist, and Russia is a planned economy. With almost negligible though interesting exceptions, the means of production belong to the state, and there is no private property. What shall be produced, and when, and in what quantities and qualities, and how this shall be distributed, is determined by the Council

[8] Preface, May 12, 1941: "But there is one group in America which has not been adequately brought face to face with the facts. I mean American businessmen." For England see Gracchus, *Your M.P.* (London, 1944), especially Ch. V and Ch. VII.

of People's Commissars and the Presidium, who are the deputed executive of the quadrennially elected Congress of Soviets. Ostensibly, by the Constitution of 1936, these are freely elected and responsible to the Congress and the people. Actually, they are not responsible to the people in the only sense in which the United States and Great Britain understand democracy, that is, in being censurable while in office, removable from office, and replaceable by others who will do the people's will. That may come some day. It is not so yet. Presidium, Commissars, and Congress are controlled by the Communist Party, which is the exclusive party in power, maintaining itself by persuasion, propaganda and, where necessary, by force.

Is this planning for socialism — that is for the maximum standard of living available given the science, the brains and energy, the capital and natural resources of the country, and for as close an approach to equality of distribution as is compatible with maintaining the continuous productive energies of the people — necessarily dictatorial?

The answer is not far to seek, and it is as available to Hayek as it is to me. It was impossible to overturn the Czarist system of Russia, which had its origins in the dynasty of the Romanoffs four centuries ago, mingled with the remnants of a Mongol conquest and a corrupt church, without the amount of force that the Bolsheviks used, or of nearly as much force as they used. The Russian peasantry — 90 per cent of the population — were serfs till 1865 and little better than that down to the twentieth century. Force was used not merely to liberate a people from perhaps the most iniquitous tyranny ever known to man, but also to break the tyranny of class over class. This was undertaken on a faulty theory, the Marxian theory, and in a wrong and damaging temper. Part of the anger with the Czarist system was applied to the conquest of power for socialist government. It would not be necessary, it would not be desirable, it would be abhorrent, in any other country than Russia in her peculiar circumstances of 1917.

Now a system of government is not to be judged exclusively by its present methods: there must be taken into account its provenance and its destination. The Russian Revolution was the grandchild of the French Revolution, whose ethos was the establishment of Liberty, Equality, and Fraternity — but not all at once — and above all, Democracy. Karl Marx, who was the Revolution's son and the Russian Revolution's father, in quest of a society of the "free and equal," sought a philosophy and an instrument whereby the French Revolution could be fulfilled, and in particular where the spontaneous good in men and women would be liberated from suppression and distortion by tyranny of class-made governments. His materialist theory of human development was made to fit his practical purpose, though we do not allege that he was insincere. We need not dwell on the labor and value theory (based on Locke and Adam Smith!), the theory of crises and increasing cleavage between more and more of the poorer and poorer, and less and less of the ever-richer rich. What is important is that he advocated the formation of a party devoted to revolution and to nothing else, which in the course of time would overthrow the exploiting class by a dictatorship of the proletariat. Then when "the classes" had been smashed, nothing would stand in the way of freedom and equality, and men at last would govern themselves and their societies justly and fairly, giving to each according to his need and taking from each according to his ability. They would learn to govern themselves without the interposition of a government or of officials. The state, far from being anything that Hayek has suggested, would actually wither away.

This is what inspired Lenin. A realization of the Marxian dream might never have been attempted, especially as Marx had postulated it, not of an agricultural community like

Russia, but of an advanced industrial society, with classes and industries, trusts, a proletariat, and so on. But Lenin's brother was executed in 1885 because he had taken part in one of the periodical plots to assassinate the Czar.[9] The Russian Revolution may perhaps be accounted for by the meeting of the mind of a boy who had lost a dearly loved elder brother and the mind of an apostle of the creed of fraternity. Lenin himself was expelled from Kazan University in 1887 for political demonstrations. His determination, his ruthless pursuit of revolution, was complete. To achieve success he conquered the liberal, temporizing, compromising groups in his party; he fought for the conviction that the dictatorship of the proletariat (which being a majority would be no dictatorship) could only be victorious if there were a dictatorship within that dictatorship — that is, if the highly class-conscious revolutionaries became the vanguard. No one else, least of all trade-unionists, would want more than minor ameliorations of their social lot. Lenin triumphed, not *with* the people, not directed *by* the people, not even with a large and steady majority of his own party.

The aberrations of the Russian system have come from two sources: Marx gave no clue how to govern once power had been won, and his followers accepted the Marxian belief that all individuals are fundamentally alike, since they all respond equally to economic conditions. Therefore the Soviet Government, anxious to justify itself to itself, treated all individuality as an excess, when individuality is really normal. Again, it was urgently resolved to raise the standard of living very quickly, and this meant rapid industrialization. And again, the land was surrounded and sometimes

---

[9] There had been an abortive one in December 1825, engineered by a large number of liberal aristocrats, and put down with horrible severity — they cannot be accused of wishing for a planned state.

penetrated by mortal foreign enemies. Finally, when men have arrived in office after years of exile, of revolutionary activity, and of the most rigorous and dangerous life — ever conscious of police spies and assassins, not absolutely sure that their comrades are not planted by the Czar's sinister detective forces — they never relax their alertness to personal danger and for their own personal safety take offensive-defensive measures which are not part of their social doctrine. Still, the origin and motivation of the system lie in the quest of freedom and equality, against the autocratic forces of the oldest and toughest of the European tyrants; while its destination — as can be partly surmised from its policy of increased prosperity, social services, social security, the right to work and leisure, the career open to the talents, and widespread education — is *not* the destination of the Nazis.

Whether the complete planning they undertake, and the speed with which they have pushed it forward, would require everywhere the techniques they use, whether the fear they inspire and the peculiar rewards and punishments they invoke would have to be used everywhere, we have no means whatever of telling. The Russians, strange as it may seem to many people, are Russians, and not Americans or British! They had no Renaissance, no Reformation, no French Revolution, no War of Independence: the Czars and the Orthodox Church ruled by iron and corruption. Their genius is visible in Dostoevski, Turgenev, Chekhov, Tolstoy, Gogol — they do not read like Walt Whitman, Henry James, and Tennyson at all.

To attempt to infer from what I have told of Russia (if that were Hayek's basis of comparison) what planning would be like in America and Britain — with a long, firm tradition of democracy, with thousands of institutions of self-government; with a general acknowledgment of the principles which should govern mankind; with free association, and a free political party system, and responsible government; with education in the humanities — is failure of the first dimension. And then, further, not to define the planning in question, its purposes, its degree of comprehensiveness, the techniques which would be used and which the Russians have not got, the gradualist nature of free agreement among the various groups, the tolerance for minority opinion and all the rest — this is to pile failure upon failure.

The failure to distinguish between the antipopular nature of the Fascists and the Nazis and the pro-popular impulse of the Soviet system — a failure of Hayek, Chamberlin, Eastman, and Eugene Lyons — is one that almost cost the democratic world its liberty. If the error is persisted in, it may yet disturb the peace of the world. For these men there is nothing to choose between the two: they are both "collectivist," they are both "totalitarian," and both deny popular liberty and the rights of the individual. Two of these men, therefore, decided against America's entry into World War II before Pearl Harbor.

Hayek says: "There are strong reasons for believing that what to us appear the worst features of the existing totalitarian systems are not accidental by-products but phenomena which totalitarianism is certain sooner or later to produce." (Page 135.) It is true that the worst features of the existing totalitarian systems are not accidental by-products: they are the continuation of the methods used by the dictators to get into power, and the methods were not democratic. Listen to Goebbels: —

> We enter Parliament in order to supply ourselves, in the arsenal of democracy, with its own weapons. We become members of the Reichstag in order to paralyze the Weimar sentiment with its own assistance. If democracy is so stupid as to give us free tickets and salaries

for this bear work, that is its affair . . . we do not come as friends nor even as neutrals. We come as enemies. As the wolf bursts into the flock so we come. [April 30, 1928.]

They were not democratic: they were of set purpose murderous, and their object, in the Nazi and Fascist case, was murderous. They did not believe in democracy or its ancestry, or its future, or its promise, or the view of human nature and destiny which gave it birth. The worst features were imported by the worst men; neither the men nor the regimes nor their "by-products" were accidents. But Hayek, myopic as ever, says: "Just as the democratic statesman who sets out to plan economic life will soon be confronted with the alternative of either assuming dictatorial powers or abandoning his plans, so the totalitarian dictator would soon have to choose between disregard of ordinary morals and failure." (Page 135.) Here is an extraordinary perversion: the totalitarian dictator disregarded the morality which controls democratic government long before he became dictator. He had to make no choice: he had already abjured "ordinary morals." So Hitler, "We spit on liberty!" and (in *Mein Kampf*) "The majority of people are simple and gullible. In every nation there is only one real statesman once in a blue-moon, not a hundred or more at a time, and secondly they have an instinctive prejudice against every outstanding genius." Or, Mussolini in 1922: "*All* is the principal objective of democracy. . . . It is time to say: a few and chosen. Democratic equalitarianism, anonymous and gray, which forbade all color and flattened every personality, is about to die." This is the essence and spirit of their polity: they reject all other things.

The democratic statesman does not hold these views; and he would not be in a position to utilize them if he did. No democratic statesmen who have set out to plan economic life have been faced with the false alternative put by Hayek.

107

There is much planning already in Great Britain and the United States, much more than Hayek likes — hence his book. The plans have worked and there has been no assumption of dictatorial powers. On the contrary, if we look into the operation of democracy we see more and more rather than fewer legislative, judicial, and popular controls over policy and its execution.

Hayek concludes, "It is for this reason [that the statesman would have to choose between disregard of ordinary morals and failure] that the unscrupulous and uninhibited are likely to be more successful in a society tending towards totalitarianism." (Page 135.) He has fallen into this mischievous and almost irresponsible error because when he says totalitarianism he classes both the dictatorships we know and *any* planning in the same class, and so attributes to democratic planning the spirit, purposes, methods, and morals of dictatorship. From this it is but a step to foreseeing coercion, minority dictatorship, "regimentation" of all life, control over private lives as over men at work, propaganda, the teaching of a single view of life, and there is also thrown in "the communism of women"! Since the dictator is determined not to fail, he will, of course, bring in the scum at the top — the hangmen.

The reason that the worst got to the top in totalitarianism is simple: it is because there the worst *make* the top. They can get to the top only where they are allowed by society to make up the top. And one of the kinds of society in which the worst get to the top because the worst are allowed to make the top is, I suggest to Hayek (and he may consult Adam Smith about this also), a society of economic individualism. These are some of the more notorious names in the past economic history of the United States: Astor, Marshall Field, Rhinelander, Elkins, Hill, Gould, Stanford, Rockefeller, Vanderbilt, Morgan, Insull, Whitney.

The English economist Marshall hoped for a time when what he called "economic chivalry" would vanquish or modify the methods of the robber baron. But these methods seem to have been continued. As recently as 1921 there was a plundering of oil resources, scandalous because the men were connected with the trusted friends and political assistants of a President of the United States. In 1934 expensive air-mail contracts between carriers and Post Office officials were the subjects of charges of corrupt dealings. The crash of the Insull empire in 1935, and the investigation that followed, showed some very unsavory activities — unless Professor Hayek believes that the worst in economic individualism is only an accidental "by-product" or that the worst is the best. And in England I notice that there is a society against the taking of bribes and secret commissions, and that its secretary is a busy man.

The Senate's 394-page Report on Stock Exchange Practices (made after two years of investigation and with twelve thousand printed pages of Hearings) may be so summarized: —

Many of the evils that were disclosed . . . were inherent in the interrelationship of commercial banking and investment banking. A great many of these evils were, however, attributable to the utter disregard by officers and directors of commercial banks and investment affiliates of the basic obligations and standards arising out of the fiduciary relationship extending not only to stockholders and depositors, but to persons seeking financial accommodation and advice. The hearings disclosed, on the part of many bankers, a woeful lack of regard for the public interest and a proper conception of fiduciary responsibility. Personages upon whom the public relied for the guardianship of funds did not regard their position as impregnated with trust, but rather as a means for personal gain. These custodians of funds gambled and speculated for their own account in the stock of the banking institutions which they dominated; participated in speculative transactions in the capital stock of their banking institutions that directly conflicted with the interests of these institutions which they were paid to serve; participated in and were the beneficiaries of pool operations; bestowed special favours on officers and directors of their banking institutions and their investment affiliates to insure domination and control for their own personal aggrandisement of these officers and directors; received the benefit of "preferred lists," with resultant impairment of their usefulness and efficacy as executive officer, bestowed the benefits of preferred lists upon individuals who were in a position to aid and abet their purpose and plans; devoted their time and effort for substantial consideration to extra banking activities and positions to the detriment of the institutions these officers are paid to serve; borrowed money from the banking institutions either without or with inadequate collateral; procured the banks' loans for other individuals to effectuate the purposes of these officers and directors; formed private companies to cover up operations conducted for their own pecuniary gain; availed themselves as directors of private corporations, of inside information to aid themselves in transactions in the securities of these corporations: caused to be paid by the banking institutions to themselves excessive compensation; had voted to themselves participations in management funds and substantial pensions: and resorted to devious means to avoid the payment of their just Government taxes.[10]

[10] No. 1455, 1934, 73rd Congress, 2nd sess.

It is, however, not surprising that Hayek does not dwell on events such as these, for he is at pains to deny on an earlier page that "just" and "reasonable" can be defined in economic matters otherwise than by means of the bargain which equals make in the market — even though in fact there are no equals.

Let us recall Chief Justice Hughes on the subject of the equality of bargaining power. The women working for the West Coast Hotel Company were in the class receiving the least pay and "they are the ready victims of those who would take advantage of their necessitous circumstances." . . . The pay was so low as to be insufficient to meet the bare cost of living, thus making their very helplessness the occasion of a most injurious competition. . . . The exploitation of a class of workers who are in an unequal position with respect to bargaining power . . . casts a direct burden for their support on the community. . . . The community is not bound to provide what is in effect a subsidy for unconscionable employers. The community may direct its law-making power to correct the abuse which springs from their selfish disregard of the public interest.[11]

The sample of economic behavior quoted above is merely one taken from the great series of inquiries that were made by Congress when the appalling economic crash of 1929 had undermined the structure of American businesses and homes, and made away with the savings of millions of innocent little men and women. The point to notice at present is that if the worst are allowed to come to the top without moderation by a rule of social obligation or standards of right and wrong, they will come to the top, and will beat out the finer natures. It would be tragic if the millions upon whom the Republic depends were misled by a theory which obscures the inherent nature of planning and by a

[11] *West Coast Hotel Co.* v. *Parrish et al* (1937), 300 U. S. 379.

false historical analysis which ascribes to it the homicidal behavior of criminals like Mussolini, Farinacci, Balbo, Hitler, Heines, Ley, Streicher, Goebbels, Himmler. Those who held power in the competitive system in Germany and Italy did not stop the scum from rising, nor were they boycotted by the businessmen of Great Britain and the United States. Indeed, banker Anzilotti explained before the Italian War Crimes Tribunal that, after all, he was only carrying out Mussolini's orders!

The character of planning by government depends on which men plan; whether they plan totally; whether they plan swiftly, whether they intend to carry out their plan hurriedly; whether it is freely assented to by a public conscious of the issues involved; whether the public retains the right of dissent and reversal; whether there is a proper machinery of governmental responsibility, whether the schemes are decentralized; whether the public representatives are well-selected — in short, whether the whole process of planning is genuinely democratic.

The thought of Hayek and those who burn incense to him springs from distrust of the people. To insinuate this distrust, he asserts, "It is *probably* true that, *in general,* the higher the education and intelligence of individuals become, the more their views and tastes are differentiated and the less likely they are to agree on a particular hierarchy of values." (Page 138. Italics mine.) What does "higher" education mean to him? Is he thinking of a select crowd of university teachers with which he is most familiar? In fact, their tastes are very similar, though I do not think that it is the education, so much as their income and professional *mores* which make for similarity. And "taste" in what respect? Principles of public good? Morality? Churchgoing? Alcohol? Music? Sex? Differentiation of tastes is almost always the product of an income and the security with which to indulge them, the crude propensities being there from birth. Is there supposed to be a relationship between "education" and "intelligence"? But the marking of 6000 examination scripts (say 400 per year for the fifteen years 1931–1945) ought to have taught Professor Hayek better than this. There are hundreds upon hundreds of men in the street, whose education stopped at the age of fourteen. Their intelligence — that is, the ability to understand complicated subjects quickly when explained to them, and to apply the principles so revealed to an as yet undiscussed situation, and the ability to decide on the main strategy of a job to be done — is easily as good as, and not infrequently better than, that of those who have been through, though hardly benefited by, "higher education." The statement is pompous hokum.

By a piece of non-logic which takes the breath away, Hayek, not now relying on observation, but upon a simple turn of phrase, then unmasks himself: "It is a corollary of this that if we wish to find a high degree of uniformity and similarity of outlook, we have to *descend* to the regions of lower moral and intellectual standards where the more primitive and 'common' instincts and tastes prevail." Notice the logical fallacy of changing his terms: a difference on *tastes* has now become "lower moral and intellectual standards." There could not be high standards shared by the mass of the people! It is among "the few" that high standards prevail, and among the many that low standards prevail! He does not want to say this blankly, but he insinuates it by this phrasing, "This does not mean that the majority of people have low moral standards [though he just said so]; it merely means that the largest group of people whose values are very similar are the people with low standards. It is, as it were, the lowest common denominator which unites the largest number of people." This nicely harmonizes with the quotations given earlier from Hitler and Mussolini about the people's baseness.

The purpose of such talk is to insinuate that the mass of the people is the more likely to be swayed by the demagogue who intends to be dictator, while the people of higher education and intelligence will not be. It assumes that mere argument can sway people in the direction of a policy they do not like, whereas it is well known that people are swayed by their interests in large measure. On this see Aristotle's *Rhetoric;* consider Edmund Burke's, "A man's circumstances are the preceptors of his duty"; read Adam Smith's *Wealth of Nations,* Bentham's and John Stuart Mill's utilitarian philosophy, and almost everybody in the world except Hayek. There is the real difference between those who have obtained a higher education and those who have acquired more intelligence.

Neither the United States nor Great Britain is afraid that the "common" people will fall into the hands of a dictator, because they have sufficient ability for use in their own democratic practices to be the democratic masters of their own popular form of government. But we know that Hayek would like to "curb" the majority. For, again, inevitably, like a doom, and like Cain's brand on his forehead, he must quote from Lord Acton, of whom it was said he regarded communion with Rome as dearer than life: —

> Of all checks on democracy, federation has been the most efficacious and the most congenial. . . . The federal system limits and restrains the sovereign power by dividing it and by assigning to Government only certain defined rights. *It is the only method of curbing not only the majority but the power of the whole people.*

What a delightful thought by one of the chief beneficiaries of higher education! And how Hayek seizes on it. But Lord Acton (overwhelmed by a German education), who spent all his life preparing to write a history of freedom but who never learned enough to write it, had his history wrong when he said the federal system limits the sovereign power.[12] In the United States it was the Bill of Rights that curbed the majority; Acton was insufficiently acute. So long as the majority have the right to amend the Constitution and, through the Executive and Congress, both popularly elected, can make known their will as to what they think to be a reasonable interpretation of the Bill of Rights, Hayek and his fellow idolators cannot avoid throwing themselves on the mercy of the people. In our time the only system of government which will give Hayek what he wants — namely, the protection of economic individualism in the extreme form that he wants it — is dictatorship, which coerces whole peoples, and sneers at rule by persuasion.

[12] *Helvering* v. *Davis* (1936), by its wide interpretation of the "General Welfare" clause, threw wide open the door to federal action over almost the whole field of legislation all over the United States.

# CHAPTER VII

# Labeled POISON

> For, when any number of men have, by the con-
> sent of every individual, made a community, they
> have thereby made that community one body, with
> a power to act as one body, which is only by the
> will and determination of the majority.
>
> — JOHN LOCKE

No Pure Thought and Drugs Act requires that a con-
coction of fallacies be labeled POISON. All the more
reason for self-control by those who speak to the public,
because the effective continuation and improvement of
democratic government requires of each citizen an attempt
to play the part of statesman and political leader.

It is not responsibility in the sense of the laws of libel
that ought to be demanded of writers for the public. Hayek
feels a kind of social responsibility, and his Preface indicates
some qualms of conscience. He says: —

> When a professional student of social affairs writes a
> political book, his first duty is plainly to say so. This
> is a political book. I do not wish to disguise this by
> describing it, as I might perhaps have done, by the more
> elegant and ambitious name of an essay in social philoso-
> phy. I hope I have adequately discharged in the book
> itself a second and no less important duty: to make it
> clear beyond doubt what these ultimate values are on
> which the whole argument depends.

There is, however, one thing I want to add to this.

Though this is a political book, I am as certain as any-one can be that the beliefs set out in it are not determined by my personal interests . . . in different circumstances [that in wartime others are too preoccupied to write] I should have gladly left the discussion of questions of national policy to those who are both better authorized and better qualified for the task.

To make the admission that "this is a political book" is an insufficient discharge of the responsibility involved in writing a political book. Much more care and scientific scruple are required if it is to occupy the status which "a professional student of social affairs" expects from fulfilling what he alleges to be a painful duty of writing.

Hayek is an economist, but in this work he is going widely and deeply into questions on which chiefly Political Science, and its more special branch, Public Administration, can give answers. I do not mean that no one but a professional student of these subjects is entitled to an opinion on the questions, but unless he had read all there is to be read on the subjects he handles, he would have no right to expect acceptance, or to widen his title from that of economist to that of "professional student of *social* affairs," or to speak with such dictatorial assurance. Nor ought those who read him to allow him any claim to an authority on matters outside his field which he may possess on matters within it. He betrays the most abject ignorance of some fundamentals which are essential to his thesis.

I refer specifically to his theories: that the Nazis sprang from the socialists; that dictatorship on the European Continent is the product of theories of economic planning; that German evolution in the direction suggested above is traceable chiefly from 1870; that the ideology and political activity Hayek lived through in Austria just before World War I must produce in Great Britain and America what they produced in Germany; and that "the Rule of Law" is incompatible with planning.

Huxley, the collaborator of Darwin, it is said read all that was written on a subject before he started writing: it may be said of Hayek that he writes all that there is to be written before beginning to read! It is a most important issue of public policy that when one undertakes to affect the public mind care shall be taken to inform it. It is surely a mistake of the first order to give contemporary humanity the impression that nature had revealed everything possible by the time history arrived at Adam Smith, and only through Adam Smith's line of descent.

The exercise of responsibility to the public requires a considerable control over the passions. Hayek operates with a Malthusian gloom and censoriousness of mankind. Malthus argued that the growth of population put an end to hopes of human progress, economically, because the growth of population must by far outstrip the productive capacities of mankind. It is material to notice at this point, in relation to Hayek, that he recommended many measures for keeping the population down, but hardly any for increasing the product of industry. The state was to be severe with relief of the poor and, to discourage them from bearing children, to encourage political economy lectures to them at their marriage advising that unless they were well-off they had better not have children. Events have since laughed the gloomy analysis and prognosis of 1803 — directed against the optimism of William Godwin — off the face of the earth. Productive capacities have remarkably outstripped the astounding growth of population in the nineteenth and twentieth centuries; in England the population has increased 500 per cent, and yet each member of this increased population has four times the wealth of his ancestors of a century ago. The United States increased its population from 4,000,000 to 131,000,000 with even greater per capita wealth.

The European population multiplied threefold, with a lesser but still a vast advance in economic wealth. But Hayek, anxious to win his case, must introduce the modern version of the Malthusian gloom.

In their wishful belief that there is really no longer an economic problem people have been confirmed by irresponsible talk about "potential plenty" — which, if it were a fact, would indeed mean that there is no economic problem which makes the choice [between one end and another] inevitable. But although this snare has served socialist propaganda under various names as long as socialism has existed, it is still as palpably untrue as it was when it was first used over a hundred years ago. In all this time not one of the many people who have used it has produced a workable plan of how production could be increased so as to abolish even in western Europe what we regard as poverty — not to speak of the world as a whole. The reader may take it that whoever talks about potential plenty is either dishonest or does not know what he is talking about. Yet it is this false hope as much as anything which drives us along the road to planning.[1]

To support his determination that the world shall not be improved he relies upon the authority of Mr. Colin Clark's *Conditions of Economic Progress* (1940): —

The oft-repeated phrases about poverty in the midst of plenty, and the problems of production having been already solved if only we understood the problem of distribution, turn out to be the most untruthful of modern clichés. . . . The under-utilization of productive capacity is a question of considerable importance only in the

[1] Hayek, *The Road to Serfdom,* p. 98.

U. S. A., though in certain years also it has been of some importance in Great Britain, Germany and France, but for most of the world it is entirely subsidiary to the most important fact that, with productive resources fully employed, they can produce so little. The age of plenty will still be a long while in coming. . . . If preventable unemployment were eliminated throughout the trade cycle, this would mean a distinct improvement in the standard of living of the population of the U. S. A., but from the standpoint of the world as a whole, it would only make a small contribution towards the much greater problem of raising the real income of the bulk of the world population to anything like a civilized standard.[2]

This passage, indeed, deals with the existence of poverty in the world and the difficulty of raising the standard of living even in the United States, which by reason of technology and other things is better placed than any other country to achieve this.

But it will be observed that Mr. Clark is referring to the phrase, the "cliché" as he calls it, of "poverty in the midst of plenty"; that is poverty *now,* not "potential" plenty, which is Hayek's stalking horse. Hayek is using Clark's denial of plenty *now* as a basis for denying *potential* plenty. Furthermore, Clark does not deny the possibility of "potential plenty." He says, "The age of plenty will still be a long while coming," but he does not say it will not or cannot come. Also, he makes an admission regarding the "preventable unemployment" and "a distinct improvement" in the standard of living of the United States. Moreover, he does not consider the use of the productive resources available by governmentally planned enterprise, but only the re-

[2] *Ibid., n.* 3, reprinted here by permission of The Macmillan Company, publishers.

sults of private enterprise hitherto. Further, Clark shows in the rest of his book that the welfare of some countries has risen immensely since 1870, partly as the result of a more deliberate attention to the question of raising the standard of living by governments, by private enterprisers, and by co-operative arrangements made among individuals (notably in Denmark), supported by the state arrangements regarding education and technical preparation and credit facilities.

In other words, Hayek has misused a sober and sad generalization about the *present* system of production to deny the possibility of future improvement.[3]

It is not the present purpose to argue that an economic millennium is to be crowded into tomorrow. But it is equally far from political veracity to dash cold water over not only generous hopes but also the inventiveness to which such hopes give rise, by the perversion of a simple statement. What is wrong is the attempt to make a case by distortion: it is not good for the public weal, or for the maintenance of a liberal democracy, to use tactics of this kind. It deludes both those who want progress and those who want to stand pat, and so incites each against the other. Mr. Clark, it will be seen, still leaves the door to hope open; Mr. Hayek viciously bangs it shut.

Mr. Clark is at pains to show the dependence of national income upon productive capacity. Is it to be denied that governmental guidance, fiscal policy, and government enterprise can help to raise the national income in advanced

[3] For example the Brookings Institute's study, *America's Capacity to Produce*. Professor Joseph Schumpeter in his *Capitalism, Socialism and Democracy*, p. 65, goes even further with his judgment that an increase of production giving $1300 *per capita* is perfectly feasible in the United States by 1978, that is little more than double what it was in 1928, and at 1928 prices, and with a population of 160 million.

economies and are practically indispensable in developing backward economic regions such as Jugoslavia, China, and India? Illustrations are: domestic raising of capital and the direction of its use — in the provision of the basic productive and warehousing equipment (warehouses to preserve harvest product), processing factories, cold storage; in better technical methods of winning forest products, sorting, saving, and using improved seed; in roads, irrigation works, soil-erosion defenses and soil recuperation; in railways; or the raising of capital abroad, somewhat in the manner foreshadowed in the Final Act regarding the United Nations Bank of Reconstruction and Development.[4]

Hayek picks on a *concept* rather than a working system of economics, and then uses the concept as though it were not a figment of the intellect but the actual system. The method is what Walter Bagehot called "a simpler imaginary man."[5] It is especially dubious when used by a writer who later affirms that there are economic and social happenings that the public cannot be expected to acknowledge as it is incapable of understanding them.[6]

This is the tactic. Say that *if* there is private enterprise based on freely individualistic and completely competitive economic operations without any state direction, and *if* all the gains and the losses are the exclusive rewards and punishments of the private economic operators, the greatest economic good of all society results. From this draw all the conclusions by a process of deduction about the value of the resultant freedom: the pleasure coming to each individual, the care which each will take to satisfy the wants of others because only by doing this efficiently will all be able to make a profit, while if they do not, others who are in competition for the market will drive them out of the oc-

---

[4] *Cf.* Finer, *Economic and Social Council of the United Nations* (World Peace Foundation, 1945).

[5] Bagehot, *Economic Studies* (1895), p. 97.

[6] Hayek, *op. cit.*, p. 204.

cupation by superior efficiency. Add all the rest of the deductive squeezings which can be obtained from a premise which already contained the conclusions. Then pretend that there is nothing — well, hardly anything — wrong with this system, even as an exercise in logic, and then with only an occasional insignificant doff of the cap not *to*, but *at* the facts, give the illusion that this phantasy is what is in operation. Call this "liberal" planning, or planning by competition.

After this ideal picture has been offered, draw a picture of the opposite extreme and convict it by calling it planning against competition. (Lippmann uses this tactic also.) Imagine society as an organized and conscious group managing *everything;* the individual has nothing whatever to say in the determination of ends or methods; society's purposes are not *his* purposes; the state is not only complete in its embrace of all matters economic, social and political, but resolute to the last punctilio of having its own way . . . attribute all cruelty to it. At that point exhibit the two concepts, and remark, with a leer, what a tremendous difference there is between them, and suggest again (for the suggestion has already been wrapped up in the point from which the start was made) how much more wealthy and easy man can be in the first state of society than in the second!

The trouble is that neither is an existent state of society; they are only states of mind — Hayek's mind. Real society has never been operated on the model which is represented in the individualistic instance, nor could individualism operate unassisted (as Hayek must afterwards admit). Nor has there ever been a society like the "collectivist" one he puts forward — not even in Nazi Germany; of course not in Italy, and certainly not, even in the most collectivist state of all, Soviet Russia. Even plain common sense, without immersion in libraries, is likely to teach that a middle way is found by actual human beings.

Hayek's only known humor is to have inveighed orally

against the "muddle-headedness of trying a middle way." The middle way, however, Aristotle's Golden Mean, is the way that most people arrange their public and, indeed, their private lives. It is not a question of adding together the two extremes and dividing by two, to obtain a middle way. It is a question of choosing, combining, and applying a number of principles, none of which in fact may be the *complete* system in the mind of the person, and then asking, of all these many urges and principles which surge up in us, "Which combination will give us the greatest satisfaction with the least burden, long-run being weighed with short-run?"

Of all the nations in the world prone to middle ways or a "mixed" system, the British and the Americans are foremost. Indeed, it is the permanent and standard reproach of the English way that it is "muddle-through."

In international recriminations this trait has even appeared as "hypocrisy." But what does it mean? It means that the Americans and the British are the empirical people beyond compare. They are experimental. All their philosophy is tentative and experimental, even of those writers like John Locke, Adam Smith, John Stuart Mill, and A. V. Dicey, who are misunderstood by Hayek, yet quoted as though they supported his case. They do not proceed from one major premise all the way down, or up, the doctrinaire view, but work now with one principle and now with another, squeezing something from each, and tacking along an "illogical" line. Think of the weaving in and out of the Justices of the United States Supreme Court! Yet the citizens of these countries live and thrive and feel free.

Henry Hazlitt in the *New York Times* was misled by Hayek's claims into believing that he understood the English character, though *The Road to Serfdom* was given far less respect in Britain than in the United States. Mr. Hazlitt said: "It is a strange stroke of irony that the great British liberal tradition, the tradition of Locke and Milton, of Adam Smith and Hume, of Macaulay and Mill and Morley, of Acton and Dicey, should find in England its ablest contemporary defender — not in a native Englishman but in an Austrian exile."[7] Does Mr. Hazlitt, in the presence of so strange a phenomenon, not smell a rat? For Hayek is no exile and we shall show, as we have already shown, that Hayek does not understand the English tradition.

Hayek does not consider the making of a middle way from the inside of the minds and characters of those who operate the economic and political system. Those who by acting in association make the system such as it is in practice, with all its features and subtleties, are omitted. He looks at a "system" from the *outside*. Again and again, it is suggested that planning will be imposed in the name of a single objective which is alien to the masses of the people who are to work or live under it. This is to leave out the inner psychology of the movement towards planning, and so to mistake its speed, drift, direction, and proportion. The essence of "liberalism" is experimentalism and the middle way, and its nature is to be discovered in practice, which means in the actual minds of actual people in a phase of history. Omitting this experimentalism is to introduce into the political ways of the Anglo-Saxon peoples a method, a temper, and a want of moderation and measure hostile to their liberalism. Graham Wallas, the essence of the best of Victorian England, thirty years ago advised against pitting absolutes against each other, and urged that "quantitative" methods — that is, *how much* of each principle? — be used to guide public policy.[8] Degree, not Logic, is the vehicle of human advancement.

*The Road to Serfdom* is based on the belief that economics is severable from the whole field of government and

---

[7] *New York Times Book Review*, September 24, 1944, p. 21.
[8] Graham Wallas, *Human Nature in Politics*, Ch. V.

morality. Economics is but a part of human nature, and not the whole of its integument, whether vertical or horizontal.

For two thousand years and more the grand problems upon which Hayek dilates have troubled the mind and the conscience of scores of philosophers. There is at hand a body of knowledge in electoral, parliamentary, party, administrative, and judicial practice which makes nonsense of his gloomy, indignant negative on state activity. Experience has revealed the range of incentives that keep men at work and inventive, and that conduce to obedience to the government. All this study decidedly offers a justifiable belief that a far higher degree of economic welfare is available for all, with liberty not diminished to a dangerous degree, if measures of production, distribution, adjustment, and initiative are organized through parliamentary statute and effected through responsible executive and administrative action. To act as though such research were not available is not fair to those whom he has encouraged not only to cherish an illusion, but also to act upon it in the critical time ahead.

He also asserts that though men can be trusted to conduct without guidance or regulation the difficult operations of modern large-scale business, they cannot as citizens be trusted to make laws to supplement, guide, or even supplant these individual activities. We deduce from this that men have neither the capacity nor the right to allow their general moral outlook (which determines the amount of effort they actually spend upon economic acquisition) to put their economic activities under the more general regulation of themselves as associates in the nation through government. Although he argues that governmental control over the economy means control over a man's will, because it is exerting a control over his income and his means of acquiring it, he is unwilling to admit that control over other people directly by those who possess economic power may

126

have the same effect. Indeed, it may be worse, for concentrated control which may be easily located may offer the opportunity of calling the wielder of power to account for his use of it. But where it is dispersed, under the antiseptic name of "private enterprise" or "economic decentralization," society would be incompetent to trace down every act of coercion exercised by those in control of employment. The Federal Trade Commission records testify to that. Somehow, when the private enterprise system ruins a man it is impersonal; but when the government passes and enforces a law it is personal! He assumes that contract and property are parts of impersonal nature, whereas it is an ancient story that they are made by law.

It is a part of this curious perversion of insight that the growth of "liberty" (which, like "freedom," is not defined) is not attributed to the growth of liberalism and the influence of philosophy, or to habit-breaking geographical discoveries, or to the contemplation by the human mind of the alternatives that lie before it as the experience of the centuries exhibits a long gallery of different pictures of felicity and opportunity to man. According to Hayek it is not a Wycliffe or a Huss, a Luther or a Spinoza, or a Jack Cade, or barons against a king, or a gibing Voltaire, or the rediscovery of Greek science and politics, or a Copernicus, that shatters an ancient cosmology and dissipates the terror of hell. It is not the thought of Rousseau, or the psychological theory of John Locke, that produces rebellions against authority and builds a liberal theory. It is *commerce* which produces free government and liberal ideas! And this he easily converts into commercial men who lived in the rich cities of Northern Italy, and in Amsterdam, Hamburg, London. Of course, merchant princes and businessmen have played their parts, but Hayek has confused the creation of great ideas and their popular support in the more populous places with the patronage and hobbies of the wealthy — as in the Medicis' encouragement of the arts. What, according to history, was the role of the businessmen? To negate the state; or as purveyors of contracts with it to exploit it; or as licensed monopolists to manipulate its power for their own ends, even to grinding down native populations in colonies or to conducting the slave trade. Or not to be taxed by the monarchy without representation in parliament. Or, as Professor Tawney and others have shown, to pervert the Christian doctrine, and pretend that theirs was a heavenly morality, a religiously supported accessory to their unbridled propensities to make a fortune. There was a parliament in England centuries before these commercial developments in Italy and Holland.

Hayek acknowledges that "individualism" grows "from elements provided by Christianity and the philosophy of classical antiquity," and was "first fully developed during the Renaissance." But he swiftly rushes away from the influencing of whole societies by these forces, incidentally not in the interests of economic individualism, but as he says, in "the respect for the individual man *qua* man, that is, the recognition of his own views and tastes as supreme in his own sphere, however narrowly that may be circumscribed, and the belief that it is desirable that men should develop their own individual gifts and bents." (Page 14.)

But we cannot consider man *qua* man as an isolated Crusoe with no social dependence and no social obligations and without a Church. It is impossible to conceive of the supremacy of a man's tastes being unlimited, if they are noxious to others. Few people would concede a full right of revolution to any one man, or a few, or a larger minority. Are there *no* limits to the very desirable purpose of developing individual bents and gifts?

How have these questions been answered, and how can their answers be further developed? *Only* as a process of give and take and of developing compromise in the sweep

128

of time, by the combination of *all* the elements of man's mind and character, and not merely the economic.

To Hayek the thousand years of striving is summarily disposed of. It is a function of the economic drive.

> The gradual transformation of a rigidly organized hierarchic system into one where men could at least attempt to shape their own life, where man gained the opportunity of knowing and choosing between different forms of life, is closely associated with the growth of commerce. From the commercial cities of northern Italy the new view of life spread with commerce to the west and north, through France and the southwest of Germany to the Low Countries and the British Isles, taking firm root wherever there was no despotic political power to stifle it. In the Low Countries and Britain it for a long time enjoyed its fullest development and for the first time had an opportunity to grow freely and to become the foundation of the social and political life of these countries. . . . The conscious realization that the spontaneous and uncontrolled efforts of individuals were capable of producing a complex order of economic activities could come only after this development had made some progress. The subsequent elaboration of a consistent argument in favor of economic freedom was the outcome of a free growth of economic activity which had been the undesigned and unforeseen by-product of political freedom.[9]

It appears then that there were already at least two nations where there was "no despotic power" *before* commerce brought the notion of "individualism."

The crucial term in this extract is the word "associated." It is like the words that Karl Marx uses to relate the forces

[9] Hayek, *op. cit.*, p. 15.

of production to the prevailing ideas and the governmental system (as "rooted in the material conditions of life" or "the economic structure of society — the real foundation on which *rise* legal and political superstructures," etc.) so that one never exactly knows whether the former is a cause of the latter.

If "associated" here is not causative, the rest of the passage has little meaning; if it is causative, it is false history. "No one can deny that the cause of the prosperity of this city is the freedom granted to those who trade there" — thus the foreign merchants in Antwerp to Philip II in a protest for continued liberty in the middle of the sixteenth century. Real history shows that certain groups captured the state for both general and economic liberty, and those interested in the latter forced back or seized the state so that they could enrich themselves. The state was not a natural development arising out of some spiritual order to which all, rich and poor, powerful and lowly, were submissive. The free rise and fall of the economic successes and failures were aided and prevented respectively by control of the instruments of the state. The power thus acquired was used to enforce and perpetuate the status in society arrived at by economic success. Indeed, if Hayek consults Adam Smith's *Wealth of Nations* he will find that it asserted from history that those who had acquired property set up civil government in order to protect it. We need proportion.

The sovereignty of the old order was not taken over by the masses, though mass appeals were made, but by the few whose interest it was to establish doctrines and laws making the world "liberal" for *them*.

In those centuries during which the doctrine of "individualism" was developed and propagated and fought for, there were few if any who considered "individualism" to be anarchy. The change to be made was from a sovereignty

st still be government, for the economic impetus
s not productive of spontaneous harmony or the
ce of competition without tears. Nor is man with-
deeper society-shaping needs such as justice, hu-
nd equality; these can crash the economy, and
be subverted or not helped by the economy.

iety is to remain democratic, that is, to have the
political direction in every respect in the hands of
e, to continue with periodical elections of legisla-
executive (the guarantee of freedom), to undertake
tions with good temper, with free political parties,
dom of association, and to hold its officials to strict
ility, neither Marx nor Hayek can be taken as its
The true American and English tradition of the
ay, with acceptance of the political maturity of the
, including its wise men and skilled practitioners,
cial heritage of spiritual and governmental con-
t move forward with economic initiative according
se of the desirable and the feasible, and its sober
e in the ways and means at the disposal of its
ental apparatus.

are six classic economic errors which Hayek must
way, before anyone should accept his dogmatic and
assurances. They are nineteenth- and twentieth-
heories, and, like Hayek's, are all on the gloomy
there are today more people in the world, they live
ney live more healthily, and they are in general
than one hundred and fifty years ago. These errors
Adam Smith's Iron Law of Wages and his labor
Value; (2) the Malthusian theory of Population
inishing Returns; (3) Ricardo's theory of Rent;
arxian prognosis of Increasing Misery and Increas-
mulation in Two Classes; (5) the theory of the
f Money; (6) the theory of the Trade Cycle.
auty of economic theory is only skin-deep. Yet it is

that was not controlled by the whole, to a sovereignty that
would be controlled by all individuals together.

It is useful to dissolve Hayek's dependence upon the authority of the Englishman, John Locke. Locke's political
theory embraces five main foundations. First, men cannot
live without society and settled government. Second, the
supreme ruler of that society is the Legislative, "sacred and
unalterable in the hands where the community have once
placed it." Third, every man puts himself under an "obligation to every one of that society to submit to the determination of the majority, and to be concluded by it." Fourth, the
purposes of government are to preserve the life, liberty, and
fortunes of the citizens; and these shall not be taken away
without their consent, but that consent is "the consent of the
majority which can do anything." So long as there was a
periodically elected legislature "to decide the rights of the
subject by promulgated standing laws and known author-
ised judgments," the rule of "absolutely arbitrary authority
was excluded," and the "obligations of the law of nature"
which lay upon legislators, that is, "the preservation of mankind," were fulfilled. Fifth, the amount of property which
has the claim to be protected by society should be limited to
what can be made use of "to any advantage of life before it
spoils." Can anyone engross as much property as he will?
There is a decided, No! "The same law of nature that does
by this means give us property (which you have put your
labour into) does also bound that property too. . . . Whatever is beyond this (the amount you can use without spoiling
for your own use) is more than his share, and belongs to
others." (Chapter V, para. 31.) "That little piece of yellow
metal [the invention of money] enabled men to carve themselves too much — which was useless as well as dishonest."

It is abundantly clear that John Locke has no message for
economic individualism. Individualism raised difficult prob-

not wished to pull away the props of our confidence in economists, but to see that they become more worthy of it. Economists have made great errors which have had practical application in government and business policy — in rent laws, poor laws, land tax laws, public works policy, *laissez faire* when there should have been state assistance. Matters would have been worse if more people had submitted to the economists' theories and if men of common sense had not taken a balanced way and treated each case on its merits — an act abhorrent to Hayek who, in one passage, objects to dealing with cases on their merits.

Economists have promulgated their theories as though they possessed the authority, force, and completeness of Nature. Yet they have been wrong.[10] Because their capacity to distinguish what was of local and temporary importance from what was of essential and constant significance was weak, like that of most human beings, they were not without their prejudices, and even their interests, in wishing that certain things could be accomplished which they had very much at heart. They were wrong because they could not control their logical faculties, and they were wrong because of a simple inability to obtain all the material facts required for a valid generalization. Yet they were unwilling to be tentative.

Human volition could not stand against their impetus. They always spoke in a completely sanguine tone, as though they were privy to the designs of Nature herself. There was one school of economists, the physiocrats, from whom Adam Smith acquired a number of fallacies, who went so far as to propose that government should do nothing at all except teach the whole population at the public expense "the principles of the natural order."

[10] Suddenly, in 1935, in his *General Theory of Employment, Interest and Money,* Mr. Keynes upset them, and especially Mr. Hayek.

The nostalgia for the past is tremendous: the past could do no wrong, the present is slipping — and as for the future, it has already slipped. Locke, Adam Smith (even when he sanctions *public* enterprise, because *that* is part of authoritative teaching), John Stuart Mill (who is of a very different mind altogether from Hayek) and others are worshiped by the reactionaries. But there is a complete absence of homage to contemporary Englishmen and American economists and political scientists: J. M. Keynes, Sir William Beveridge, the Webbs, R. H. Tawney, Joan Robinson, Alvin Hansen, and Wesley Mitchell. Worship of the past gains of society is acknowledged: thus the "division of labor" was "tumbled on." (Page 50.) Why cannot man go on "tumbling" to even better devices? Is not government, with its ability to draw on the talent of its own and other lands, and to undertake investigations and the discovery of information entirely impossible to any other organization or individual, very likely to "tumble" rather well? Is there not even a case for trying? Mr. Hayek still declares: "No."

# CHAPTER VIII

# The Engineer's Dials

> The world has never had a good definition of
> the word "liberty," and the American people just
> now are much in want of one. We all declare for
> liberty; but in using the same word we do not all
> mean the same thing. . . . Plainly, the sheep and
> the wolf are not agreed upon a definition of the
> word "liberty."
>
> — ABRAHAM LINCOLN, *Baltimore,*
> *April* 18, 1864

Without exaggeration we can summarize Hayek's
creed as follows: "Economic activity is the innocent exercise
of brain. Political action is the guilty exercise of power.
Economic enterprise is merely the beneficent use of knowledge. The action of governments is the application of
coercion. Economic competition is the exercise of freedom
in choice of ends for all individuals. The action of the state
imposes its ends on individuals by force." Hayek has a fixa-
tion on the "individual" as the original and sovereign factor
in the production and distribution that make up the economic process. The millions of isolated individuals enter
into a community by competing with each other, in the
supply of all goods and services, and so produce organization
and order. The fittest survive, come to the top, and develop
new forms of wealth. This, he thinks, is productive of the
highest economic good. Since the essence of competition is
freedom of choice by each individual consumer and pro-

ducer, it not only produces better than any alternative the maximum wealth (all the individual products added together), but promotes the maximum of morality, for morality is the opportunity to make wrong choices and the will power to make the right ones.

Hayek elects to call this creed "Economic liberalism." He dissociates himself, formally, from *laissez faire;* but actually he is approving *laissez faire,* since his "economic liberalism" is opposed to the co-ordination of individual efforts by the state. It regards competition as superior, not only because "it is in most circumstances the most efficient method known but even more because it is the only method by which our activities can be adjusted to each other without coercive or arbitrary intervention of authority." (Page 36.) "Indeed, one of the main arguments in favor of competition is that it dispenses with the need for 'conscious social control' and that it gives the individuals a chance to decide whether the prospects of a particular occupation are sufficient to compensate for the disadvantages and risks connected with it."

Hayek asserts in this way that it is *individuals* who are the factors in the competitive process. But whether he means *ones* or *groups* is not answered, and that is a serious issue since in actuality in this process the *ones* have hardly any power at all. Hayek is blind to the fact that "authority" or "coercion" has often come from the successful competitors, and that competitors have actually possessed themselves of "arbitrary authority," and even established and shaped the state in order to do this. Study of the activities of coal mine owners in either Great Britain or the United States would provide dozens of illustrations.

Does competition give all individuals a chance to *enter* the occupation of their liking if they have the manifest economic ability, and economic ability only? What happens when nearly 25 per cent of the nation's jobs are shut down? Hayek does not answer.

The elegance and innocence of competition are reinforced by certain beauty prescriptions furnished by Hayek.

He says: —

> It is necessary in the first instance that the parties in the market should be free to sell and buy at any price at which they can find a partner to the transaction and that anybody should be free to produce, sell, and buy anything that may be produced or sold at all. And it is essential that the entry into the different trades should be open to all on equal terms and that the law should not tolerate any attempts by individuals or groups to restrict this entry by open or concealed force. Any attempt to control prices or quantities of particular commodities deprives competition of its power of bringing about an effective co-ordination of individual efforts, because price changes then cease to register all the revelant changes in circumstances and no longer provide a reliable guide for the individual's actions.[1]

Is the system of competition by "individuals" then as innocent as it seems to be? "Open or concealed force . . . Any attempt to control prices . . ."! How can this be, if competition is self-actuating order? Hayek is worried by something operative *inside* the competitive system itself — so strong, indeed, that he must contemplate the intervention of government to restore competition; that is to overcome force with force.

So the innocence and beneficence that Hayek is imputing to competitors, and with which he is seducing adherents, are blown away! The contemplation of something beautiful which happened in the golden state of nature when rare Ricardo lived and wrote gives place to the problem of the degree of strength the government should use.

[1] Hayek, *The Road to Serfdom*, p. 37.

One other tribute to the innocence of competition ought to be considered: —

> In a competitive society the prices we have to pay for a thing, the rate at which we can get one thing for another, depend on the quantities of other things of which by taking one, we deprive the other members of society. This price is not determined by the conscious will of anybody. And if one way of achieving our ends proves too expensive for us, we are free to try other ways. [*If we have the means, and if others use no coercion.*] [2]

In modern societies, the division of labor is highly complex. Production is conducted by producers who *specialize* in some occupation or craft or process or simple operation on the assumption that the partial products will be brought together to form a whole and that the market will be the place where consumers and producers settle what shall be produced and exchange the contributions with each other. Division of labor enables the maximum return to be obtained from all the factors of production.

There was hardly a time in human history when the division of labor was not practised. It flourished especially when cities grew up. Why then a kind of paean of triumph about it from Hayek, and even more from Lippmann? They both look upon it as a miracle: Hayek as a miracle "tumbled upon." Their purpose, I think, is to suggest that this condition of a high standard of production has been rationally developed by competitive forces since about 1800, and that such a miracle of rational subdivision could not be performed by a government setting broad economic tasks for the community. If therefore society wants a high standard of living it should continue with the *free* system of

[2] *Op. cit.,* p. 93. Bracketed remark is mine.

division of labor. This outlook neglects a parallel subdivision of labor going on in the public services of the government. It is impossible to imagine that any government would have everything done by one man for the whole community! The co-ordination of the specialized productive activities which is now supposed to be brought about by the operation of the market could be replaced by government policy over the subdivided occupations and the full expression of consumers' choices.

For the division of labor to function well, what is required, says Hayek, is: —

> . . . some apparatus of registration which automatically records all the relevant effects of individual actions and whose indications are at the same time the resultant of, and the guide for, all the individual decisions. This is precisely what the price system does under competition, and which no other system even promises to accomplish. It enables entrepreneurs, by watching the movement of comparatively few prices, *as an engineer watches the hands of a few dials,* to adjust their activities to those of their fellows. The important point here is that the price system will fulfil this function only if competition prevails, that is, if the individual producer has to adapt himself to price changes and cannot control them. The more complicated the whole, the more dependent we become on that division of knowledge between individuals whose separate efforts are co-ordinated by the impersonal mechanism for transmitting the relevant information known by us as the price system.[3]

There is an *if* in the picture which may be made real by supposing real conditions. Suppose the geographical distance between the price makers and the price watchers is very

[3] *Op. cit.,* pp. 49–50. Italics mine.

great, great enough (quite apart from overseas distances) to defy anticipation or readiness to act upon their indicatory meaning; and suppose (which raises important problems) no concert between the many contributory producers for the same market; and suppose (which raises more anxious problems) the want of prior knowledge by the purchaser of the variation of quality in the items so priced, and the inability to rely upon the warranty of quality — is Hayek not in an unreal position to be talking about the engineer watching the hands of a few dials? The engineer's dials do register constant units; do Hayek's prices? The only guarantee that they will go on registering the same units must come from someone exercising conscious control for the benefit of all — that is, the government.

Some people, even though they are aware of price registration, will not take the action which the price registration would require to maintain a system of perfect competition. Others cannot.

Some, like Fiske, use the price of wheat as a guide to monopolistic rather than competitive practice. Others, who are hungry, may be unable to act because the price may be above their means. It is not a good argument against planning action by a government that here are beautifully impersonal price registrations, without questioning the likelihood, which can be tested by the history of particular markets, of their being effective.

Does any operator, large or small, remain satisfied with price alone, even on the Stock Exchange, which is closest to Hayek's price registration? The enterpriser is constantly trying to get behind the prices in the market, because if he waits until they register he will be too late to do business profitably. He looks beyond to the forces which are in control of his prices, that is to say, to the forces of supply and demand. He wants to detect the future conditions that will determine the price at which he can buy and sell. He does not trust to the prices of the moment, otherwise there would be nothing dynamic in his enterprise. The economist at the Chicago stockyards is always watching out for the prospects of the harvest of corn. There are many conditions that he cannot know in a widespread division of labor, and the more subdivided, the greater the number of prices. In fact, only governments can know what all the prices, in a sum, prove. The Rome Institute of Agriculture was necessary because the "individual" entrepreneur found the index of prices too heavy an instrument to handle. Cartels are, in part, a response to the intolerable burden of anxiety on "individual" operators, waiting to act according to a price that will be set for them. They cannot bear the suspense; and they cannot act in time, at the end of the process. In very large fields of economic activity, could not government do the better guessing than even the most extensive private organization?

Ludwig von Mises[4] started, Hayek[4] exploited, and Walter Lippmann[4] has manipulated the theory that when all goods and services are produced and sold by the government, and there is no competition among producers and the consumers cannot show their preferences, prices cannot exist. In this case there can be no "economic calculation" by the government regarding what to produce, when to produce and where to sell, and therefore no index by which to distribute labor and capital.

Governmental equivalents to competitive pricing[5] are demonstrated, however, by the manipulation of ration values according to changing supply and demand and by the supply of government capital to the river and hydroelectric authorities. The only difference between the indices of

[4] Cf. Ludwig von Mises, *Socialism,* Part II; Hayek, *Collectivist Economic Planning,* Ch. III and Ch. IV; Lippmann, *op. cit.,* pp. 94–95.
[5] Cf. Robert Hall, *Economic System in Socialist State;* and

Hayek and planned prices is that the former are freely distortable by economic individualists without public responsibility while the latter would be decided by responsible "public-business-men," with clear instructions and clear lines of responsibility for the use and abuse of their authority.

Hayek's main thesis that there is nothing so efficient as competition and the price system to advance the wealth of mankind depends on the system of private property.

> So long as property is divided among many owners, none of them acting independently has exclusive power to determine the income and position of particular people — nobody is tied to any property owner except by the fact that he may offer better terms than anybody else. . . . What our generation has forgotten is that the system of private property is the most important guaranty of freedom, not only for those who own property, but scarcely less for those who do not. It is only because the control of the means of production is divided among many people acting independently that nobody has complete power over us, that we as individuals can decide what to do with ourselves.[6]

It is not irrelevant to observe that not only is property an important guarantee of freedom, but that murder, falsehood, bribery, theft, breach of faith, and the power of imprisoning other people are also guarantees of freedom. Yet society has set bounds to them.

The most pertinent issue arising out of Hayek's declaration is this: Does the present distribution of property in any country represent the contribution made by the native

A. P. Lerner (a pioneer in the field) *Economics of Control* (New York, 1944); and Meade and Fleming, "Price and Output Policy," *Economic Journal,* December, 1944.

[6] Hayek, *op. cit.,* pp. 103–104.

ability, uncoerced, without fraud, without inheritance, to contribute to the economic product of the whole of society? If the answer could be affirmative, I would be content to rest the matter here.

The curve of the distribution of incomes Pareto constructed shows that the income of a nation is far from equally distributed and its sharp inequality is rather the same for all western countries. Part of the difference is explained by inheritance, not merely of "property" in the abstract, but productive equipment such as land, shares in enterprises, and patent rights. This creates inequalities which are the product of the past. Accumulated inheritance is not the simple product of ability to fulfill an economic function that all other equal individual competitors wanted; it is often the product of luck, of force, and of fraud. I by no means exclude ability but it is surely wrong to pretend that there is no aberration in the competitive system even when due to the passage to the new generation of property which was acquired by sheer ability.

In proposing to abolish mass unemployment, Sir William Beveridge was faced with this problem of private property, and whether it must be regarded as a fundamental right. His answer (and Mr. Hazlitt of the *New York Times* should know there is no doubt he is an Englishman) is that there is no right to own the means of production. He says: —

The list of essential liberties given above does not include liberty of a private citizen to own means of production and to employ other citizens in operating them at a wage. Whether private ownership of means of production to be operated by others is a good economic device or not, it must be judged as a device. It is not an essential citizen liberty in Britain, because it is not and never has been enjoyed by more than a very small proportion of the

British people. It cannot even be suggested that any considerable proportion of the people have any lively hope of gaining such ownership later.

In this respect he speaks like Mill:—

The laws of property have never yet conformed to the principles on which the justification of private property rests. They have made property of things which never ought to be property and absolute property where only a qualified property ought to exist. They have not held the balance fairly between human beings, but have heaped impediments upon some, to give advantage to others: they have purposely fostered inequalites, and prevented all from starting fair in the race.[7]

And Mill emphasizes that the distribution of property came from conquest and violence, and "still retains many and large traces of its origin."

Clear convictions of this kind will not be found in *The Road to Serfdom*. Hayek's strongest observation is: "It is by no means sufficient that the law should recognize the principle of private property and freedom of contract; much depends on the precise definition of the right of property as applied to different things." (Page 38.)

Thus Hayek is not helpful to his readers; he fails to differentiate between forms of property which promote and those which obstruct the wealth and freedom of all. Instead, he finds it more convenient to ascribe to "planners" and "collectivists" and "socialists" indiscriminately, and without qualification of speed or purpose, the abrogation of all private property. When the reader is then nonplused, the way is open to Hayek to inveigh against tyranny, which has nothing to do with the problem to be solved.

[7] *Principles of Political Economy*, Bk. II, Ch. I, Sect. 3.

146

As a matter of fact, and this is one of the abysmally dark fields in Hayek's neglect of the study of government in practice, systematic studies of property have been proceeding for at least a century in the United States and Great Britain. There are, literally, hundreds of studies of particular aspects of property in relation to specific problems and reforms. In the United States every congressional or departmental investigation into an economic problem, in Great Britain every Royal Committee of Inquiry over the last hundred years, has in some way or other touched on the issue of the form of private property and its justifiability and value in relation to that particular problem of economic life. The major premise is that private property shall be the basis. Then the investigators proceed to determine what ought to be the legal and enforceable limitations on the use of this property, and how it will affect other sectors of the economic and political life of the country.

Thus, for example, the law does not allow an owner to build where he likes, or as high as he likes. It does not permit inflammable and shaky structures, however profitable they would be for the exploiter of the property. Factories and workshops can only be built in certain locations, and recent public investigations (as the Report on the Location of the Industrial Population in Great Britain) contemplate the power of the state to designate where industry may be located. Property cannot be used as it suits the owner as against maximum hours legislation. Agricultural land must be kept clean and drained. Money cannot be lent except under terms stated by the law. Bills of exchange are heavily subject to law. There is a legal responsibility for the destruction of the waste products of a workshop, and for the pollution of rivers. The state has established control over the charges and conditions of warehousing certain goods — for example, butter. It is illegal to sell tainted food, and it is subject to inspection and condemnation, though it is private

147

property. The sale, the renting, the leasing of property, are subject to government regulation. Bequest is shaped by the law. Basic industries like railways, communications, mining, have come under government regulation. Property in cattle is subject to laws for control of animal disease — as owners had no compunction about selling and buying them, to the public's damage. And then there are all the businesses "affected with a public interest," like grain elevators, stock exchanges, milk, public carriers of all kinds, insurance, packing companies, and employment agencies. Society is all the better for these and other limits.

The many decisions of the law courts arising out of the constitutional guarantees, or Bill of Rights, trace the principles of property, especially cases arising out of the Due Process clauses and those related to the Police Power, Taxation, Eminent Domain, and the General Welfare. It is not possible in this context to begin to demonstrate anything of the care and ingenuity with which the courts have tried to reconcile the economic and other liberties of the individual and the liberty and the other needs of *other* individuals and society as a whole. The flavor of their attempts must be suggested by a quotation from one of the most sensible of justices — it is at once a reproach and an admonition to Hayek and those deluded by him. It is the dissenting opinion of Mr. Justice Holmes in *The Hudson County Water Board v. McCarter* (1912):—

All rights tend to declare themselves absolute to their logical extreme. Yet all in fact are limited by the neighborhood of principles of policy which are other than those on which the particular right is founded, and which become strong enough to hold their own when a certain point is reached. The limits set to property by other public interests present themselves as a branch of what is called the police power of the state. The boundary at which the conflicting interests balance cannot be determined by any general formula in advance, but points in the line, or helping to establish it, are fixed by decisions that this or that concrete case falls on the nearer or farther side. For instance, the police power may limit the height of buildings in a city, without compensation. To that extent it cuts down what otherwise would be the rights of property. But if it should attempt to limit the heights so far as to make an ordinary building lot wholly useless, the rights of property would prevail over the other public interest, and the police power would fail. To set such a limit would need compensation and the power of eminent domain.

It sometimes is difficult to fix boundary stones between the private right of property and the police power when, as in the case at bar, we know of few decisions that are very much in point. But it is recognized that the state, as quasi-sovereign and representative of the interests of the public, has a standing in court to protect the atmosphere, the water, and the forests within its territory, irrespective of the assent or dissent of the private owners of the land most immediately concerned.

There is, in fact, then, much going on in the world unknown to and unsanctioned by the reactionaries.

Let it not be forgotten that property only gives freedom because the law allows it to. It is the law alone which can give freedom protection, and this depends solely on the law-abidingness of the majority of society. Hence what freedom a man may have is the product of the good sense and average conscience of all his neighbors. Nor would the use of property mean a thing, unless the law protected contracts. The business world would be a scene of carnage and cannibalism if there were no law of contract which was state-enforced.

According to the reactionary manifesto competition is both blind and impersonal, and both of these qualities have good results: —

> It is not irrelevant to recall that to the ancients blindness was an attribute of their deity of justice. Although competition and justice may have little else in common, it is as much a commendation of competition as of justice that it is no respecter of persons . . . rewards and penalties are not shared out according to somebody's views about the merits or demerits of different people but depend on their capacity and their luck.[8]

Notice the trick of logic of allying competition with justice; and introducing a goddess! Let it also be noticed that the blindness of Justice was contrived in order that she might hear better, and without bias by a pretty face or by the menacing frowns of the powerful, or the pitiful plea of the weak. It was in order to weigh both sides, and *not* to exclude any of the claims put forward by the suppliants. Economic individualists are actually so awake to their own interests that they distort competition by the use of force, fraud, and coercion. Hayek believes that the operation of competition is impersonal, that is, that nothing but a consideration of economic good affects the economic person, and that he is therefore willing to abide by the economic influence of other people's valuations of his services to them, no matter what his own economic acquisitiveness or other motivations may be. This is not true to life. It is a fact that competition bears its own destruction within its own merits. The failure to understand this is as bad an error as that of Karl Marx in regard to the theory of economic value. Marx affirmed that value depended on the amount of labor in the commodity. He noticed, however, that the price of some

[8] Hayek, *op. cit.*, p. 101.

150

commodities is many times greater compared with other commodities in the market than the amount of labor required to produce them: the usual example is diamonds. *He failed to study the exception* or account for it. If he had, he would have found the price is closely related to its *appeal* to the purchaser. Likewise, if Hayek had meditated longer, and without prejudice, on the *failures* of competition, he would have found that almost universally among rich and poor alike, employers and employed alike, free-lance and salaried worker, they spring from protest against the human insufferability of competition as a general rule of economic production.

The Ohio Supreme Court said in its decision fifty years ago, outlawing the Standard Oil Company (49 Ohio, 137), "By the invariable laws of human nature, competition will be excluded in the interest of those connected with the combination or trust." And the reason why this is so was indicated by Chief Justice White, when, in 1907, the American Tobacco Company was dissolved because its acts demonstrated from the beginning "a purpose to acquire *dominion and control* of the tobacco trade" by methods "ruthlessly carried out upon the assumption that to *work upon the fears or play upon the cupidity of competitors* would make success possible." [9]

Hayek says, "It may be bad to be just a cog in an impersonal machine; but it is infinitely worse if we can no longer leave it, if we are tied to our place and to the superiors who have been chosen for us. Dissatisfaction of everybody with his lot will inevitably grow with the consciousness that it is the result of deliberate human decision." (Pages 106–107.) Need it be pointed out that the public authority in charge of employing applicants for jobs would operate according to a standard, not arbitrary or made by itself? Of course,

[9] *U. S.* v. *American Tobacco Co.,* 164 Fed. 700; 221, U. S. 106 (1911).

there would be free choice by the applicant according to ability and inclination.[10] It shows a determination to be blind to suggest that in the system of competition, *as it is,* decisions are not made by persons for persons and about persons. The maximum explanation may be offered that the work has dried up; or that there is no longer a market; or a customer has gone bankrupt; or that there are better applicants. But nobody is there, no principle prevails, to make sure that there is no intrusion of a personal as distinct from a market interest in the decision.

The state, and there are already many enterprises run by the state, or the municipalities, or public corporations, must meet these issues also. If the citizen can understand the explanations offered by the competitive business man, he can understand those of the state as business manager and employer. More, he could be a little more certain that the official employing him has no absolute, unreserved, unprincipled tenure and power, but a qualified and answerable one.

We now arrive at a further absurdity. . . . "The power which a multiple millionaire, who may be my neighbor and perhaps my employer, has over me is very much less than that which the smallest *fonctionnaire* [11] possesses who wields

[10] Professor A. C. Pigou, in a sweet-tempered review of Hayek's work, cannot avoid chiding him for his statement that the individual person seeking work would not be free in state-directed industry: he observes that, of course, the state would be only concerned to determine the *numbers* in each occupation.

[11] This French word is used in preference to the American "public employee," or the British "civil servant," as a sly way of suggesting something foreign and sinister, and to divert the mind from the obscure but suggested "bureaucratic" temper and methods of the French civil service, perhaps under the autocratic regimes before the Third Republic. It is to smear the problem with a foreign brush that was at one time — before democratic control — not too clean.

the coercive power of the state and on whose discretion it depends whether and how I am to be allowed to live or to work." (Page 104.)

This does not represent the practice, let us say, of the personnel division of the Tennessee Valley Authority, the administration of Boulder Dam, the action of an official of the United States Employment Service, the insurance activities of an official in the local employment exchange under the British National Insurance Acts supervised by the Ministry of Health. Yet some millionaires — for example, the Astors, the Vanderbilts, the Rockefellers, the Jay Goulds, the Leland Stanfords in their time, and others — arbitrarily "fired" their "hands." It is known also that English agricultural laborers were intimidated by their employers and landlords, and that the secret ballot had to be instituted to protect the voter from economic retaliation.

However, Hayek alleges that the power of the state is coercive: —

> To split or decentralize power is necessarily to reduce the absolute amount of power, and the competitive system is the only system designed to minimize by decentralization the power exercised by man over man. . . . What is called economic power, while it can be an instrument of coercion, is, in the hands of private individuals, never exclusive or complete power, never power over the whole life of a person. But centralized as an instrument of political power it creates a degree of dependence scarcely distinguishable from slavery.[12]

If we submit Hayek's conviction of the pure decentralization of economic power to the test of common everyday observation, these questions become awkward to answer, and Hayek does not make the attempt. (1) Is economic

[12] Hayek, *op. cit.,* pp. 140–146.

power (and it must be *power,* or it is incapable of producing anything) really pulverized, or is it existent in large and therefore more powerful units? (2) If it happens to be in large units, is this a necessary thing in contemporary and future economic enterprise? And, if so, is there then a case for the intervention of the government to avoid the results of overmighty force, to stop the "barons" and "royalists" from dominating "the little men"? (3) Is it, when so decentralized, capable of producing as much as if it were supplemented and, in the appropriate cases, supplanted by public enterprise? (4) Is it not possible to decentralize the power of government — is it, indeed, not already what is achieved in the practice of government? (5) Are there not many other institutional devices to prevent the action of government from being oppressive and to keep it accountable? (6) Why should more rationality and honor be attributed to millions struggling with each other economically, than to the millions democratically composing their own laws and controlling their responsible administration? If Montesquieu and the fathers of the American Constitution, facing this question, could answer it with the separation of powers within the government, why need Hayek answer it by excluding from the governmental field most of the activity ties of mankind that he regards as important? From Alexander Hamilton to the days of Hayek stretch one hundred and fifty years, and men have discovered and applied firm and fruitful devices, that Hayek knows not of; and even then, the devices depend on the continuing support and good sense of the men.

It is no accident that the system of economic competition leads steadily to centralization within the economic field itself; while in the state, centralization has been accompanied by the recognition of the need for decentralization and the practical establishment of it. Mussolini tried to convince me during an interview that the decrease of municipal self-government in Great Britain since the time of John Stuart Mill meant that Great Britain was becoming less democratic. I asked him whether it were not true that even with all the work of government consolidated at the center of a state there would still be a full democracy if associations, parties, the press, the parliament functioned freely and vigorously, and if the executive were responsible to the legislature, the people. He goggled and gave no answer. For that is the real problem. And Hayek gives no answer.

I do not recall a mention in *The Road to Serfdom* of one of the oldest and most dependable of the economists' friends: the long run. But it is one of the assumptions of competition. If the system goes on and on, then in the long run the incompetent producers are beaten out, and the competent take their place. New and better processes will replace inferior ones. Inventions will outdate less acceptable machines and products. Even monopoly may be smoothed out by new competitors ganging together, or the market may change to a new article as a substitute. Those who have their factories shut down will gather credit and start again as demand picks up, or may go off into other lines. The worker out of work will turn to something else, or move to places where there is work to be found. Thus, all will be for the best in the best of all possible worlds — if we are patient and wait. The unbalanced economy will return to equilibrium. All we will then see is prosperity — and some debris. The trouble with this theory is that the debris consists of men and women. In order not to be debris, they refuse to wait for the long run; and so all bankers, manufacturers, merchants, farmers, and workers — all — set up rigidities against being debris, that is against the long run. There was a time when the capitalists, being in full possession of the state, whose militia was at their service, could dissolve the rigidities of other people. Now the workers, as well as they, declare with J. M. Keynes: "In the long run we shall all be dead." Hence they all chisel into competition. They want security, not competition.

Even if Hayek's pawns moved perfectly, which they are very far from doing, there would still be something lacking in his principles of statecraft. He can win his game only by omitting the conscience of the community.

# CHAPTER IX

# The Engineered Dials

> The behaviour of the community is largely
> dominated by the business mind. A great society is
> a society in which its men of business think greatly
> of their functions. Low thoughts mean low be-
> haviour, and after a brief orgy of exploitation low
> behaviour means a descending standard of life.
> — A. N. Whitehead

What has now to be said has been long known, and
it is widely understood: private enterprise is not innocent;
it is guilty and sick. This is known to Hayek and the busy
disseminators of his views. He is not illuminating the
qualities of enterprise, but darkening and hiding its mortal
deficiencies. He does battle for competition, but he cannot
defend competitors. It is to the latter subject that he should
really address himself.

There are at least six maladies from which private enterprise suffers. These are: —

1. The Inequality of Property Ownership.
2. The Control of Industry by Large Corporations.
3. Monopolies of Production and Labor.
4. The Suppression of Invention.
5. The Inefficiencies of the Market.
6. Mass Unemployment.
7. Despoliation of Other Economic Enterprisers.

## 1. The Inequality of Property Ownership

The ownership of property in the United States is so unequal as to upset the balance between economic effort and ability on the one hand and production, compensation, and consumption on the other. This is largely the result of inheritance, and it directly implies a distortion of what the mass of human beings want and could obtain from their country's productive effort as compared with what is actually produced and distributed, because only the wants of those who have means are effective as demands for goods. This is a grave distortion of the wealth of nations.

Some figures indicate its severity. The present argument does not depend on the minute exactness of the figures, but on the broad relationship of inequality of distribution revealed.[1] A calculation for 1930[2] shows that 2 per cent of the population own between 40 and 45 per cent of all private wealth, leaving 98 per cent of the population with 55 to 60 per cent; and that the top 1 per cent of the population possesses 59 per cent of all private fortunes. Estimates made by W. I. King, for 1922, showed that about two thirds of all the wealth belonged to about 10 per cent of the population, or in other words that one third of the wealth belonged to about 90 per cent of the population.[3] For the end of 1928, King showed[4] that only about

[1] There is no up-to-date, comprehensive, and definitive analysis of property distribution, in spite of the many millions of dollars spent in economic research. *Cf. Studies in Income and Wealth,* Vol. 3, National Bureau of Economic Research (New York, 1939), Parts One and Two.

[2] Lehmann, in Ch. 9, p. 161, *Political and Economic Democracy* (ed. Ascoli, New York, 1937).

[3] *Ibid.,* p. 161.

[4] Table XII, p. 13, *Burroughs Clearing House, Sept. 1931,* used by Tresckow in estimating trust-business possibilities.

3,500,000 owners, or one thirteenth of them all, owned about 10,000 dollars each — the rest of the population was below this level; and nearly 14,500,000 owners had over 5000 dollars, leaving about 32,000,000 owners with between nil and 5000 dollars. Again, he showed that about one third of all the wealth is owned by less than 3 per cent of the owners, each with above 100,000 dollars. Owning above 20,000 dollars each, there were only half a million people, and together they owned about 47 per cent of the total. And some 20,000 owners possessed more than a million dollars each, making altogether about 13 per cent of the wealth.

We need do no more than adduce some further illustrations of inequality from an investigation made in 1923 by the Federal Trade Commission.[5] Taking samples of estates submitted for probate, the Commission showed that about 11 per cent of the estates (under 500 dollars each) represented only one five-hundredth of the total value of the estates probated; that one thousandth of the estates, however, represented 8.5 per cent of the total value; and that about one fortieth of all the estates (above 100,000 dollars) comprised nearly 46 per cent of the total value. Now, the latter figures do not exactly represent what the heirs received; yet, since they represent estates of deceased persons, they indicate the enormous disparity in the passage of wealth to the new generation.

Enough has been said to demonstrate two things: (a) the enormous inequality of property and (b) the gaping disparity of inheritance. The first (a) means inequality in opportunities of economic enterprise and saving, and the second (b) implies the functionless inheritance of contemporary wealth and opportunity, the receipt of unearned income, and in many cases candidature for absentee owner-

[5] Federal Trade Commission, *National Wealth and Income;* Senat. Doc. No. 126; 1926, p. 59.

ship of a share in corporate economic enterprise. As inheritance taxes in the United States begin only at 50,000 dollars, while in Britain they begin at 500 dollars, and as the British began this form of taxation as far back as 1894, while in the United States Federal Inheritance Tax started in 1916, the proportion of inherited property in the United States is probably at least as great as in Britain, as estimated presently.

There is all too good ground for Hayek's suggestion that more serious attention should be paid by the state to the laws of inheritance. But he himself does not do it, and his sudden friends have not yet begun a passionately zealous campaign for it in the legislature. This inequality vitiates his assumptions about the beneficent efficiency of the price index.

As for incomes, the computation made by Brookings Institution for the year 1929 summarizes their inequality. "About 21 per cent of the families received only 4.5 per cent of the income. The 11,653,000 families with incomes of less than 1500 dollars received a total of about 10,000,000,000 dollars. At the other extreme, the 36,000 families having incomes in excess of 75,000 dollars possessed an aggregate income of 9,800,000,000 dollars. Thus it appears that 0.1 per cent of the families at the top received practically as much as 42 per cent of the families at the bottom of the scale." [6]

In the United States (1935-1936) more than 6,700,000 families and single individuals, comprising 17.01 per cent of the total, received annual incomes of 500 dollars or less; over 18,400,000, 46.54 per cent of the total, received incomes of 1000 dollars or less; roughly 32,000,000, or 81.82 per cent of all, received annual incomes of 2000 dollars or less. The total amount of income drawn by about 18,500 families and single individuals whose annual incomes were each 50,000

[6] Cf. *America's Capacity to Consume*, p. 56, Brookings Institution.

dollars or more was about equal to the total income of the 6,700,000 families and individuals with each an income of 500 dollars or less. The total amount of income drawn by the 177,600 families and individuals with each an annual income of 15,000 dollars and above was about the same total as that which went to the 12,600,000 families and individuals receiving annual incomes of 750 dollars or less.[7]

In addition, wealth and family fortune give only a few the education and training necessary for occupations. These, therefore, are highly paid because of the shortage in the supply of labor.

The Brookings Institution investigation computed for 1929 showed 42.1 per cent of the national income to wages; 21.7 to salaries; 6.8 per cent to farmers; while rent, interest and profits, and other property incomes received 28.1 per cent. The figures for the succeeding years show a slight improvement for nonproperty incomes.[8]

For Great Britain it is reliably computed that before the war about 70 per cent of incomes above surtax level were unearned; and that no less than three quarters of this unearned income is inherited;[9] that probably between two thirds and three quarters of the national capital is inherited at any given moment.

These figures are the minimum necessary to refute the innocent trust which Hayek and his followers seem to have in the incomparable and unsurpassable contribution of individualist competition to national wealth. The door to occupations and to promotions to the highest ranks therein is closed to talent and energy as it should not be, because education is not equally accessible to all talent capable of benefiting.

[7] Cf. *Statistical Abstract of the United States,* 1939, p. 313.
[8] Cf. National Resources Committee, p. 380.
[9] Josiah Wedgwood, *The Economics of Inheritance,* pp. 44, 234.

We can only get goods and services if we can pay for them; and they will only be produced if a demand backed up by the power to pay comes into being. So far as production is responsive to demand, and not carried on at the whim of the producer, which might land him in ruin should he guess badly, or a fortune if he can tempt us, the consumer is a sovereign power. Hayek's friend, Ludwig von Mises, is fond of saying the action of the consumer is rather like a referendum continuously in operation. But the crucial question is: do all men have equal votes in this perpetual ballot? If they had, they would not vote for the satisfaction of the same wants, for the same services and for the growing and manufacture of the same commodities, for there are differences in taste. But where there is such a degree of inequality, the productive system and the variety of the occupations are thrown violently out of relationship to the basic wants of both rich and poor, not supplying enough to the latter, and supplying much in excess to the former.[10] The fundamental trouble is that the productive resources of the nation, its capital, its land, its skill and labor, are allocated by a biased referendum, where the voting power is weighted in favor of the upper income groups. The economic voters, as it were, cannot choose the candidates (because big corporations can dictate supply) and have unequal voting power — some of the productive units under free competition can never be voted out of office in spite of too high costs of production or prices, or bad quality of service. (It may occur to the reader that the logical conclusion of the economic competitive system would be to restore property qualifications for voting.)

What is the possible meaning of price in this system, or the value that is put upon the labor of the various occupations? All consumers together are determining the level and

[10] The very rich can make such large savings that they are even no longer tempted to invest.

of or into the grade. There is much "hereditary" transmission of occupation. "There is . . . apparent a fairly close agreement, in general, between the family circumstances and occupational status of fathers and the ultimate occupational attainments of sons." The movements upwards are little more than a few steps — because, in the factory, skilled men from the schools come in at the higher levels, the "growth in the size of business enterprise with its requirement of large aggregate of capital limits the opportunity of a worker to become his own boss." [17] Though it is difficult to predict the inheritance of ability, we are prepared to assume that inherited ability accounts to a substantial degree for the inequalities of fortune noted above, yet can Hayek deny that occupational distribution is grossly perverted by inequality of fortune and education based on family resistance to competitive individualism?

All Hayek has to say of educational and occupational opportunity is that, if the state were to control entry into jobs, the state would be too mechanical in its establishment of entrance tests, and so the intensity and persistence of those who did not show ability at the outset would never be rewarded, as now happens (note!) by future opportunities. This is an entirely gratuitous supposition.

## 2. *The Control of Industry by Large Corporations*

Hayek's rapture over individualism is based on pure legend because it is not in the nature of competitive individualism that individualism shall exist and operate for the multitude. The majority is excluded. The pristine state-of-nature spontaneity of millions of entirely separate, will-

[17] *Cf. Economic Theory and Correct Educational Distribution, 1931,* p. 69, cited. *Education and Economic Well-Being in American Democracy* (the educational Policies Commission, Washington, D. C., 1939), V, p. 121,

ing individuals has been overtaken by large-scale organization. There are coagulations in the circulation.

In the United States there were, in 1937, between 10,000,000 and 12,000,000 economic units. These employed about 48,000,000 people, whole or part-time. But of the total economic units, nearly 7,000,000 were farm units; nearly 20,000 were government units. Business units numbered only 1.7 million. The rest were chiefly service and professional units and very small, individually owned independent units. About one third of the total employed worked in the 9,000,000 to 11,000,000 units employing 1 to 5 persons. Almost as many people worked in units employing from 6 to 299. From 9 to 12 per cent worked in units employing from 300 to 999 each. From 12 to 16 per cent worked in units employing from 1000 to 9999 each. From 11 per cent to 14 per cent worked in units employing 10,000 and over each. In other words, from 65 per cent to 70 per cent of the employed were engaged in units of from 6 to 10,000 employed. From 32 to 42 per cent were engaged in units of from 300 to 10,000 and over; and these figures are serious understatements of the largest units, because subsidiaries of a parent corporation, as for example General Motors Corporation, are not consolidated into one unit.

Where are the "atomistic" individuals, upon whom Hayek lavishes praise? If, for good technological and psychological reasons, such "atomization" is possible, it should be made clear to Hayek's idolators what these reasons are, and that competitive individualism is only an abstraction, not a reality.

The Bureau of the Census, in 1939, reported that corporations constituted 51.7 per cent of the total enterprises in manufactures, and these employed 89.4 per cent of the workers and produced 92.6 per cent of the total value of manufactured goods, and were responsible for 92.3 per cent of the total value added by manufacture.

168

Some other data are material, though they traverse the same facts. Of the 200 largest nonfinancial corporations, one half are railroads or utilities. The former operate about 90 per cent of the railroad mileage of the country; the electrical utilities account for about 80 per cent of the electric power production, and more than 90 per cent of the telephone facilities. The remaining 107 corporations of this class include 84 primarily engaged in manufactures, 10 in merchandising, 9 in mining and 4 in miscellaneous activities. About one third of the manufacturing plants of the United States are operated by the 100 largest manufacturing corporations. The proportion of assets of all nonfinancial corporations held by 200 of the largest of them was in 1929 47.9 per cent and in 1933 54.8 per cent.

Finally it is estimated [18] that the following products are controlled to a decisive degree by one or a few companies — thus: aluminum 100 per cent, by one company; automobiles 86 per cent, by three companies; beef products 47 per cent, by two companies; candy 90 per cent, by three companies; cigarettes 80 per cent, by three companies; iron ore 64 per cent, by four companies; plate glass 95 per cent, by two companies; safety glass 90 per cent, by two companies; steel 60.5 per cent of capacity, by three companies; whiskey 58 per cent, by four companies; and zinc 43 per cent, by four companies.

All these facts are available to Hayek and von Mises. But the path-breaking researches and analysis of Berle and Means, making clear beyond all doubt the public significance of the high concentration of economic power, have meant nothing whatever to Hayek. The gist of their research has been repeated often in public discussion, but it

[18] Adapted from Temporary National Economic Committee, "Part 1, *Economic Prologue*," p. 137, Fainsod and Gordon, *Government and the American Economy* (New York, 1941), p. 18.

must be repeated again here. The 200 largest corporations in the United States control 50 per cent of the total corporate wealth of America, and they made two thirds of the new capital offers between 1922 and 1927.

Where, then, are the thousands — nay, the millions — of independent individuals, highly decentralized, unable to coerce or be coerced, and subject only to impersonal forces?

Berle and Means show that the nominal control of the direction of the 200 corporations is vested in some 2000 different men, and that, of this very small group in control of the economic use of so great an economic empire, a large part are inactive, with, therefore, only a "few hundreds" of separate individuals in control. Fifty per cent of the corporate wealth of the nation in the hands of about one thousand men! No state except Soviet Russia, surely, has even attempted this degree of centralization.

The corporate form of organization is a legal creation of the genius of capitalist enterprise, for the purpose of making business enterprise less risky than it would have been if the contributors of capital had been fully liable in all their possessions for any failure of their business. The corporation and joint stock company laws principally limited liability of the contributors to the declared amounts of the capital ventured. This was to attract, and it did attract, small investors. But they contribute to another of the failings of "economic individualism."

They, the owners, who according to Hayek are economic venturers, finish their venture, in fact, at the moment they have bought their shares; for thereafter the law and the technical facts of the business are quite beyond them. Their power, which was to be impersonal and contribute so to the excellence of the competitive process, has gone. It is no use for the idolators of competitive enterprise to say that the small shareholders could, if they wished, continue their economic control by withdrawing their capital and investing it elsewhere, or attending meetings to criticize management. They cannot do it. The terms of the law of company meetings prevent it. Secondly, the public opinion of the whole meeting against a troublemaker is overwhelming, unless the company is about to go on the rocks and the shareholders are able to see them. But, thirdly, the complexity of the businesses run by a modern corporation is almost always far beyond the shareholders.

It might still be answered that they can get advice from stockbrokers. But these men are themselves not always sure of their position. For, contrary to what Hayek says he believes, they require much more than the mere pricing dials to watch. They look at the economic conditions; they talk about the character of the men managing the enterprise; they try to judge the general spirit of the government of the country. And they are apt to be wrong. If the economy were conducted by the state, it also would manage the economy in great corporate forms like the T.V.A., the Maritime Commission, the New York Port Authority, or like the Central Electricity Board, or the London Passenger Transport Board in Great Britain. I do not say in exactly the same form; I have in mind at the moment the scale of organization, rather than the internal form of administration. The state can be tolerably certain that the information about the business and its practices and policies given out by its officials would be honest because based upon a form decided by elected representatives of the public with accounts and discussions open to publicity. The antiseptic of mismanagement is Publicity, but it is hard to sell any quantity of it to men with an appetite for Hayek.

*The owner has become passive.* No longer, as in Adam Smith's simple conceptions for a very small village-local agricultural market economy and domestic manufactures, does the owner make decisions based upon his personal will, his ideals, his morality, and his direct knowledge of the immediate circumstances. Real responsibility has disappeared. Listen to him talking politics! and especially discussing Russia, which does not allow this kind of thing! The divorce of ownership from responsibility and control has already given rise to the notion of a dictatorship of the Managers — James Burnham, its author, argues that it is already here, and even that it is desirable — a queer reversal of Hayek's position. Burnham agrees that capitalism is very unlike the private enterprise that Hayek alleges is in operation. He attributes to capitalism two paramount features: it is composed of great corporations with absolute ownership which vests the control and disposition of property in a class of managers, and, secondly, it cannot handle the problem of mass unemployment. He believes that the first characteristic will be consummated by the entire domination of the state by a self-perpetuating class of managers, which would establish a single political party to provide the semblance of democracy and as a compensation would solve the unemployment problem. It is striking that those who found Burnham's thesis acceptable are almost unanimously those who are now devotees of Hayek.

How much more vivid and sensitive and continuously interested are the millions of voters in their political organization whether local or the central organs of the state! There is a suggestion by Hayek that once the voters have voted, their interest and power in the operation of government cease. He echoes in this respect Rousseau who, two hundred years ago, declared that when every five years the English electorate had cast its vote its sovereignty was in abeyance until the next election. Though that was two hundred years ago, and democracy was in its infancy as compared with today, Rousseau was wrong then, and Hayek is crassly wrong now. The modern voter maintains his control — how some politicians and economic individualists

172

wish that he did not! — and those controls over the operations of government are continuous in the United States and Great Britain. He has his local representative; he has his political associations; he is activated by other interested organizations. When the subject matter concerned is "above his head," he is assisted by a constitutional arrangement: an opposition which unremittingly criticizes and questions the administrators *in public,* so that the facts come out in a form which the voter can understand.

Hayek is much shaken by the portent of the large-scale firm. As it does not conform to his theory, it is very awkward, although in fact it is the simple, natural product of the acquisitive man in a system of competition, not moralized or controlled by the action of the public in the form of the state, with too small a brain to handle these intricate, sprawling processes and markets.

It is easy to imagine what the hard-headed competitive men behind the clock think of Professor Hayek in front of it, watching the dials!

### 3. *Monopolies of Production and Labor*

Monopolies in the United States were established by willful men determined to build for themselves an empire over certain sectors of the field of production and distribution. There is no space available for distinctions between the various forms of pools, gentlemen's agreements, trusts, consolidations, communities of interest, holding companies, mergers, and perverted trade associations. The common purpose is well enough known: to control so much of the business that competition cannot affect price, output, methods, cost of production, and efficiency and quality. The history is too plain for its significance to be missed. Standard Oil, American Cottonseed Oil, National Linseed Oil, National Lead, Diamond Match, American Tobacco, Distillers' and

Cattle Feeders' (known often by its other name, "the Whiskey Trust"), International Harvester, United Shoe Machinery, American Sugar Refineries, National Biscuit, Du Pont, United States Steel, Alcoa, National Cordage, and Amalgamated Copper are some of them. There were great scrambles for control over oil, the railroads, gas, and electrical power by resolute adventurers, together with seizure of land, with the same effect. Transport, communications, banking and credit, were also absorbed and dominated by concentrated groups.

At all costs the reactionaries must deny that monopoly is the inevitable result of the competitive spirit itself. Hence an alibi must be found. It is, naturally, found in the place where it would most hurt any case for government direction or assumption of the businesses. Hayek denies that monopoly is a result of technology which would make large-scale business more efficient than small-scale. The proof adduced by Hayek for this view is an excerpt from the *Final Report* of the Temporary National Economic Committee: "Nor do the economies of size invariably necessitate monopoly. . . . The size or the sizes of optimum efficiency may be reached long before the major part of a supply is subjected to such control. The conclusions that the advantage of large-scale production must lead inevitably to the abolition of competition cannot be accepted." To what, then, is monopoly due? It is to "collusive agreement" "and promoted by public policies." Hayek's mind simply will not assimilate this, and he slips away from the issue, saying that the progressive growth of monopoly during the last fifty years "is simply the result of the policies pursued in most countries." The "policies pursued in most countries" could be the policies pursued by businessmen; or the policies pursued by the government, which could mean either positive action taken by the government to foster monopolies, or not taking action to pursue and disperse them.[19] I will go on directly from where Hayek has so conveniently left off. This is what he omits from the quotation from the *Final Report:* [20]

In those industries where the nature of the product, the market, the supply of materials, and the technology of production is such as to encourage it, competition reasserts itself in the face of collusive agreements and restrictive legislation. In other fields the characteristics of the produce, the market, the supply of materials, and the technology of production are conducive to monopoly. But monopoly cannot be attributed to natural factors alone. It is the product of formal agreements and secret undertakings; of combinations, inter-corporate stockholders, and interlocking directorates; of the ruthless employment of superior financial resources and bargaining power; of unequal representation before legislatures, courts, and administrative agencies; of the exclusion of competitors from markets, materials, and sources of investment funds; of restrictive contracts and discriminatory prices; of coercion, intimidation, and violence. It is the product, too, of institutions of property which permit private enterprises to take exclusive title to scarce resources; of franchises, permits, and licenses which confer upon their holders exclusive privileges in the employment of limited facilities and the performance of important services; of patents which grant to their owners the exclusive right to control the use of certain machines and processes and the manufacture and sale of certain goods; of tariffs and state trade barriers which exclude

---

[19] *Cf.* p. 315 TNEC Monograph No. 21 with its conclusion: "In nearly every case in which monopoly persists, it will be found that artificial factors are involved."

[20] P. 90.

outside producers from domestic markets; of legislation which limits output, fixes minimum prices, and handicaps strong competitors; and of the inadequate enforcement, over many years, of the laws that are designed to preserve competition.

Hayek rushes away from these truths. He seeks to prove from American and German history that the cause of monopoly is public policy! His truculent argument is actually so shocking in its evasion as to sadden any believer in social redemption by scholarship. He says (Page 46): —

If they [the decline of competition and the growth of monopoly] were the result of technological developments or a necessary product of the evolution of "capitalism," we should expect them to appear first in the countries with the most advanced economic system. In fact, they appeared first during the last third of the nineteenth century in what were then comparatively young industrial countries, the United States and Germany. In the latter country especially, which came to be regarded as the model country typifying the necessary evolution of capitalism, the growth of cartels has since 1878 been systematically fostered by deliberate policy.

The deliberate effrontery of this argument is heightened by the fact that from this point onwards not another word is said about the United States excepting, a little further on the same page, to say "The development of Germany, however, more than that of the United States, came to be regarded as representative of a universal tendency. . . ." That is all. It is certain that to all who were bred outside Austria and were fed on anything but German books or who looked westward instead of inside Central Europe, the United States was the great teacher in the matter of trusts and monopolies. Why does Hayek remain silent about American developments, which were amazing? Because the monopolies were the product of collusion, and coercion, and often the most dishonest tactics on the part of economic individualists — not excluding physical violence, blackmail, the shutting off of information, the beggaring of competitors until they were coerced out of the trade, at which point the monopoly could then fleece the public. And also because the American Republic, being a free state, a democratic state, was able to revolt against this monstrous strangulation, and by laws and administrative action to attempt to put down these strong-arm methods. That is a point which truth should have compelled Hayek to admit to himself and to pass on to his readers.

The methods of fostering cartels· in Germany were tariffs, and direct and indirect inducements on the part of the state — but these last two methods were foreign to the United States. *Germany was not a nation with democratic responsible government.* The Imperial Government was a coalition of irresponsible landowners and heavy industry. The middle class sections, the workers, and the farm interest exercised no such power as they did in the United States. The monopolists and the government were one and the same thing in Germany; and there was no way, short of revolution, to overcome this. In the United States (and in Great Britain),[21] when the mighty shout of the people went up,

[21] The position of monopolies, from the standpoint of public policy towards them, is only slightly different in Great Britain. And monopolists in Great Britain have been less predatory than in America. But there is no such law as the federal Antitrust Act. Monopolies are held in check tenuously by the power of the courts applying the Common Law, against restraint of trade and agreements against the public interest. But even without the encouragement of a protective tariff, there was a substantial development of monopolies in cotton, bleaching and dyeing, chemicals, soap, spirits, tobacco, steel electrical equip-

the monopolists could not go on saying quite as easily as they did at first, "The public be damned!" The policy of Imperial Germany was an exploitation of the consumers by the establishment of cartels aiming at swift industrial and commercial advance for the purpose of a determined militarist foreign policy. "The suppression of competition [in Germany] was a matter of deliberate policy . . . was undertaken in the service of the ideal which we now call planning, there can be no doubt." (Page 48.) Planning for what? For war and world domination.

Fortunately, when an argument is such a travesty it

---

ment, wallpaper, at the turn of the century, especially. World War I intensified monopoly. In the 'twenties and 'thirties the depression and foreign competition in world markets caused the development of rationalization schemes in various industries, with government assistance or good will. Iron and steel, shipbuilding, textiles, various agricultural products, were so assisted, and in some cases subsidized. In other cases, like the cement, pottery, and electrical industries, cartels were established privately. The coal industry was a special case, and has necessitated practical nationalization owing to the obstinacy of the many owners in not carrying out amalgamations justified by technological reasons. Municipal authorities who are large purchasers of supplies, and whose utilities and housing operations are a field for very considerable annual investment, have for many years increasingly complained of price rings, trusts and combines. On the threshold of important social changes and a grappling with unemployment, British people have become strongly antimonopolistic. In the election of 1945, Mr. Churchill, even though the leader of the Conservative Party, was obliged to say: "We must guard against abuses to which monopolies may give rise. It is vital that there should be effective protection of the consumers' interests and of the independent businesses, whether small or large. The right remedy against harmful, restrictive practices is to set up an independent tribunal before which charges of monopoly abuse can be laid. Its work and reports should be public." And this was foreshadowed in the government's White Paper on employment policy.

178

knocks the ground from under the feet of the sophist. These are the shifts to which he is forced in order to bolster two tenets: that there is nothing wrong with competition, and that there is something wrong with the state, and therefore with all planning, regardless of its nature, purposes, and organization. If there had been no state at all while the American monopolies were growing up, there would certainly have been no state by the time they had grown up. They used every known device to destroy the state short of war: fifth column tactics, by the suborning of members of the legislatures and the law courts; debauching by bribes, drink, women, the gift of stock; control of education through control of legislatures, political parties, school committees; interference with freedom of teaching, appointments to and dismissal from university positions, the bribery of textbook writers, and many other immaculate actions of the simple, decent men watching the hands on the dial of the Engineer's Clock! They were on their way to achieving what Hayek asserts to be essential: that the state should be the assistant of the economic operators. They took the advice seriously. Their empire would have been worse than it was, and worse than it still is, if it were not for the vigorous action taken by the state!

## 4. *The Suppression of Invention*

The government gives to the inventor a patent — that is, a right of property in the invention for seventeen years. It is history, and not supposition, to say that without this protection the invention would be filched from him. By this device, society attempts to stimulate invention and discovery. The patent becomes available for exploitation by anybody at the end of the seventeen years. Society seeks these benefits in return for protecting the inventor.

The law courts have been frequently called upon to

interpret the Patent Laws, the first of which was passed in 1790, and have laid down various principles. The property right of the inventor is exclusive: he can do what he likes with his own. The faintest emphasis is laid on the view that his action should not be detrimental to the welfare of society. It has followed that the patentee is "neither bound to use the discovery himself nor to permit others to use it"!

Hence, the purpose of the law, to encourage invention for the public benefit, has at various times been frustrated, in telephones, automobiles, gasoline refining and utilization (the Ethyl Corporation case is of the richest interest), motion picture, television, frequency modulation radio, electrical equipment and lighting, road-making machinery and material, gramophone records, building equipment, rubber tires, glass bottles and containers, Pullman cars, drugs, soap, toilet preparations, cameras, razor blades, books, folding beds, duplicators, threshing machines, beryllium. The list is not exhaustive. Actions in court, either under antitrust laws or for patent infringement, prove to the hilt the antisocial suppression or retardation of the use of new knowledge, and justify the strong suspicion of similar monopolistic suppressions over a far larger field.

Yet Hayek prefers, as always, pure theory. Ignoring the stark record, he says: "The case of the alleged suppression of useful patents is more complicated and cannot be adequately discussed in a note: but the conditions in which it would be profitable to put into cold storage a patent which in the social interest ought to be used are so exceptional that it is more than doubtful whether this has happened in any important instance." (Page 203.)

The inventor usually needs capital and has not got it. He sells or leases his patent to a corporation, and this obtains a property right as absolute as his, even to the extent that it need not use the invention. The corporation's aim is to get the maximum of profit with the minimum of effort and risk. Some inventions are therefore bought to avoid adapting the existing plant and methods and personnel to compete with new knowledge. The firm can still make a profit by pursuing the old ways. Where inventions are not altogether suppressed, they are used only after the lapse of many years.

The methods are inspired. Some inventors are induced to become salaried employees of the patent-owning corporation: they are no longer free to push ahead. Many patents are bought simply as flank-protectors of patents already in use, since a single vital patent is vulnerable to competition or legal challenge. Patents are bought and intermeshed to form a barricade to progress from other quarters, and the specifications are drawn vaguely and widely to frighten off competitors. The research departments of big corporations may make enough discoveries to frustrate the more radical outsider (who would have to start from the beginning against a great active firm) and to make a claim for the renewal of license about to expire. Infringement suits harass challengers, with new processes and tools; mere threats put them out of business or make them ready to sell to or combine with the old firm. The challenger has not the money, or time, or nervous resistance to prove the legality of his claim in court: he could be ruined in a few days of litigation. The well-financed firm can prove an earlier priority in the idea: its evidence may be the vaguest, but it may be backed up by inchoate specifications put in long ago by patent counsel with foresight.

To ward off competitive new knowledge and devices from the market, the firms in possession license their machines, processes, and products by elaborate, subtle, restrictive agreements, exclusively and selectively, to clients and dealers who must respect the resale price lists and conditions for passing on the use of the machines they dictate. They have required that other auxiliary materials or machines shall be used with theirs only as they stipulate; they have prohibited the use of competitors' machines and materials; they have demanded that, instead, goods be used, which are not patented to them, to complement the use of their own patented goods. Customers who do not obey have been ostracized, and their business activities reported to the corporation by its own inspectors. Some of these procedures — for example, the "tying" clause — or dictation of the use of accessories or material, have been declared illegal. But vast corporations have prestige and an air of terror for the small man. And their lawyers have been able to compose licensing charters intricate enough to outwit the law, so long as clear duress is not exposed. Thus, liberty of contract, protected by the public, denies to the public its just heritage in expanded knowledge and improved production.

A grouping of patents is often required for the production of an elaborate article, and corporations cross-license these to each other on terms which prevent others from entering the field of supply. Their clients have no alternative to accepting the terms of the licenses; but in return they are assured that so long as they behave themselves their income will be protected by their economic overlords. Once such a structure has been set up, the corporation is master of the inventive process, government and patent laws notwithstanding: for it is too big to be challenged; it can buy inventors or crush them.

Such antisocial use of a socially provided protection — for we have done nothing but summarize the story as told in the law courts — would be of limited effect if the seventeen-year-term were maintained. But seventeen years are lengthened into perpetuity by the taking out of patents complementary to each other with staggered terms of validity.

Or a patent is asked for, and others warned off by this, and then the date of grant is deferred; and then it is deferred again by the addition of items declared to have been inadvertently omitted; and again by the addition of items declared to be new and essential.

These, then, in spite of the deductive conclusion from the profit-making motive, are the ways in which, in fact, the application and even the growth of science are restricted by modern industry. Business will take some risks, but as few as possible. It is excessively self-protective. Though stimulated by the motive of making a profit, the motive is insufficient to induce men to undertake the supreme creative tasks. The enormous risk-bearing capacity and vision of society as a whole are immeasurably superior to the timid procedures of competitive enterprise when we enter the field of the most radical scientific discoveries and their utilization for men's abundance and leisure. The age of technological groping rapidly recedes; science is swifter than business.[22]

Between July 1890 and July 1940, the United States Government instituted no less than 530 cases under the federal antitrust law. Of these cases, fifty were against labor unions.

[22] This book was in the hands of the printers when the first atomic bomb was dropped. The observations on joint research, which was so triumphant, are among the most significant in the Official Statement (*New York Times*, August 7, 1945): "But the greatest marvel is not the size of the enterprise, its secrecy, or its cost, but the achievement of scientific brains in putting together infinitely complex pieces of knowledge held by many men in different fields of science into a workable plan. And hardly less marvelous has been the capacity of industry to design, and of labor to operate, the machines and the methods to do things never before done so that the brain child of many minds came forth in physical shape and performed as it was supposed to do." After this, who again is going to pretend that the same concerted kind of attack on the making of instruments of peaceful enjoyment is impossible or undesirable?

The remaining 480 cases were against almost every conceivable kind and form of economic activity, from razor blades to artichokes, from steel, glass, gasoline, and aluminum to candy sticks, newsprint, and motion pictures. The variety of the industries and the persistence of the need to combat their monopolistic practices — and let it be remembered that the officials of the Federal Trade Commission are not all as belligerent as Mr. Thurman Arnold and they need assurance that there is a chance of conviction before they proceed to ask for it — indicate that there is something fundamental at stake.[23]

The hands on the Engineer's Dials go wrong because, to quote Plato, there is a "lie in its soul." The competitive system depends on individualism, that is admitted by Hayek. But like some other economists, inwardly recoiling from the deductive consequences of this, he immediately hastens to say that this does not mean "selfishness," known to academic circles as "hedonism." That is, man will not think only of himself when he makes an individual choice — his choice may have a very noble end: to get money in order to leave it to a university, or a church, or a library, or in order to clothe a beautiful woman or raise a family. This is granted but the choice is still made by the individual, and the power of the competitive system resides in its grant of power to the individual. This is its motive force: that he is answerable to no one for his choice, so long as he satisfies his own buyer or seller, his supplier or his consumer. If he cannot do this, then he may justly be ruined. If he can, he may rise to great fortune, power, and prestige. No one will help him; he must help himself or go under.

[23] *Cf.* the very interesting testimony of an experienced official, Corwin D. Edwards, of the United States Department of Justice, 52nd Annual Meeting American Economic Association, December 1939: "Can the Antitrust Laws Preserve Competition?"

What is wrong with this creed as a regulator of economic activity and service? Its almost universal error, the "lie in its soul," is that most men will not go down, though they may be willing to rise. They will and they do go to all extremes to avoid failure; and they will not stop to ask, "Ought I, for the sake of the wealth of the nation, or for the accommodation of my competitor, go down?" Instead they will say, and they do say: "By any means, by the sharp hook of Captain Kidd or the seductive crook of gold, I will stay where I am at least, and keep my family where it is; and if the other fellow shows a sign of beating me, I will play such a game as will hide, obliterate, subvert, and destroy his power to compete — this, or collusion with him at the expense of someone else."

The competitive system depends for its sanction on insecurity. Competitors in the real world, the men you see on the street, do not intend to be insecure. By the aid of competition they arrive somewhere above the ground floor; but once they are there, competition ceases to be a matter of moment to them. They kick down the ladder and shut the door on competitors below. It requires the power of the state to come to the rescue, not only of the men on the lower floors, but also of the general body of consumers, for they have an interest in what the competitors do to the economic machine. This desire to stay on top holds good of labor, as of owners and directors; and it makes the case more serious, for they could combine into new coagulations, joint monopolies of employers and workers, to divide society into vertical combinations, destroying on the one hand both its mass of individuals and their spontaneity, and on the other the unity of the nation and its spontaneity and independence.

Why is it that Hayek does not see these elements of human nature? First, his mind is turned where Plato, in the famous Parable of the Cave, says the philosopher's mind

185

should not be turned: away from the real world, into the dark cave illuminated from the outside, but exhibiting to the onlooker only the shadows of lifeless pottery in the shape of human beings. This is the fault of his kind of economics, and there is no defense for it. Secondly, he is blinded by an unwillingness to admit that the state can be right; hence it must be saddled with having fostered monopoly. This is nonsense — except where, as in Germany, the monopolists have secured control of the state, and the state is the defender of the consumer and indeed of other producers against the monopolists.

Men may desire fortunes, but they do not want insecurity. Security is not to be had simply by antitrust and antilabor union activities on the part of the state. And the wealth of nations depends on activities also which no individual or group of individuals can be tempted to perform. Some of these have already been suggested. It is the cupidity of competitors not the Cupid of competition that awaits Hayek's description.

## 5. *The Inefficiencies of the Market*

It is not intended to pursue the subject of the inefficiencies of the market with the thoroughness (however limited by the space for this whole discussion) of other parts of the critique of the reactionary Manifesto, but some attention must be given to it. There is undoubtedly in the argument of Hayek the constant implication that, if left to itself, the operation of the market must result in the harmony of all the producers and consumers in it. The assumption is harmony. But this is not borne out by several uncomfortable facts. A different outlook grows up among great groups of occupations or functions in the economic system: broadly, finance, and credit, manufactures, commerce, and agriculture. Each, according to the methods of economic individualism, takes its swiftest and self-interested way towards profits and security. The desire of the credit market to go slow or to go fast, for high returns and high risks or low returns and small risk, may or may not accord with the restiveness of manufacturers already in the field or of men who want to build factories and installations to exploit some invention. Those in control of credit may exert a stranglehold over all but the largest of manufactures. In Great Britain the observations of the Macmillan Committee's Report on Finance and Industry [24] showed that an unduly cautious policy of credit to home industry went hand in hand with tragic mistakes made in grasping for big returns from abroad, especially from Germany between 1924 and 1931. The United States Senate Committee on Banking and Finance in 1932-1934 made the gravest charges of a similar kind against American financiers. The British banks and acceptance houses and company promoters, working often against each other, were overanxious for gain and were negligent about the vulnerability of their credit. It must be remembered that one of the most constant and dominating features in American history is the complaint of the producers, especially agricultural, but not exclusively, that the banking and credit institutions are too avaricious and exacting instruments for the provision of capital. The problem seems to be insoluble without the provision of credit by the state. Beginning under Mr. Hoover as an instrument for the salvage of the industrial, transportation, insurance, and commercial and mining wrecks of 1932, the Reconstruction Finance Corporation took on more and more the character of the fomenter of enterprise by the grant of credit. Its policy is not only to support a common advance, but also to support counteraction against causes of depression.

The market does not operate as it is supposed to do,

[24] Cmd. 3897, 1931, pp. 99ff.

because there is at once a tendency in some of the wealthier groups to cease their intensity of exertion, and in others to create capacity to produce which is then not used. It is part of the regular psychology applied by the economic individualists that the greater the income the less the value to the individual of each additional dose. Since exertion is, on this view, undertaken for the sake of reward, the falling of the significance of the reward causes falling-off in the intensity of exertion. This is shown, negatively, by the lackadaisical attention to improvement by some of the old, well-established firms, especially British. This would not matter if corporate strategy and monopoly did not protect their slackening effort, though it still might be that they were so much better than their competitors that even the hedging was unnecessary. It would not matter much if they were not in possession of the material instruments of capital. Not only is the brain of the enterpriser not enterprising, but the workers who may be perfectly prepared to go on producing have no access to the equipment. Something of this cause has contributed to the inefficiency of the British coal mines. Most owners were too well off to have to bother by co-operative action to be better off, with the following result to the wealth of the nation: excessive separate ownership of coal wagons, large seams of coal left as a barrier between contiguous coal mines, no common policy for pumping the water out of flooded mines, no central pumping machinery.

As there is no previous and superior co-ordination of purpose and effort, and each man is watching the price dial unknown to the other, and the price indicator is as bad as we have shown it to be, a real risk, not an accurately forecast one, has to be taken by those anxious to start a venture. It is no accident that Hayek has some partiality for incomes and property based in part on "luck." A great deal of luck is required to guess accurately. The enterpriser must be quite sanguine. Professor F. H. Knight, whom Hayek rightly regards as one of the greatest living authorities on the functioning of the economic system, makes an important thesis out of the tendency of the enterpriser to overproduce after taking too sanguine a view of his luck. What seems to begin as an infallible individual choice produces collective mistakes. Wicksteed says: "Everyone benefits by a good crop of what he does grow, and if his individual crop was for any reason only an average one then his loss would be certain. . . . There is the paradoxical situation . . . the advance in well-being which we all desire and are all pursuing becomes an object of dread to each one of us in that particular department in which it is his business to promote it."[25]

This competitive and incompetent guessing at the state of mind of so many other factors in the market is, of course, part of the cause of depressions and unemployment. What it has meant in the United States is partly revealed by the existence of unused capacity to produce. The Brookings Institution has estimated that in 1929 the unused productive capacity of the United States in twenty-seven selected manufacturing industries ranged from 2 per cent in the manufacture of dairy products to 55 per cent in the manufacture of locomotives. Taking manufactures as a whole, the unused productive capacity amounted to 17 per cent of the total in 1929, and for 1925 to 1929 averaged 20 per cent. It is not worth more than mentioning the gap between these facts and the revealed extent of the unfulfilled wants, or capacity to consume, for these are obvious to everyone who travels through the countryside and the cities. Lately we have all been aroused by the number of rejections for the army due to remedial ill-health, sometimes due to malnutrition.

It is one of the most persistent and joyful experiences in a businessman's life to hurl the epithet "bureaucrat" at public servants. According to the inarticulate major premise of

[25] Wicksteed, *Common Sense of Political Economy,* Vol. 1, p. 351.

Hayek, however, the businessman is also a public servant; for Hayek praises the competitive system and the competitor's function not only because of the good the competitor does for himself but because of his contribution to the national welfare through the peculiar planning functions of competition. It appears, however, that the increase in the size of businesses, and the ability they possess to prevent prices from fluctuating sharply and to contrive that there shall be little threat of fluctuation, causes the introduction of "bureaucratic" infirmities into private enterprise. Thus, large private enterprise is charged with succumbing to habit and inertia, to subjection to complicated rules; to woodenness of response between headquarters and the field; to lack of sensitiveness and independence of mind resulting from hierarchy; to the triumph, too frequently, of seniority over fresh merit; to the reaching of the highest posts at a rather advanced age, higher usually than in the public service for roughly the same magnitude of responsibility;[26] grasping of power; and fear among the officials in the lower levels of loss of work or promotion. What is lacking in the private enterprise is that there is, except occasionally, no outside investigator who can and does compel a public examination of these inefficiencies: this advantage to the public is only available in the case of the public service. Every British postwar reconstruction scheme to come from the employers' side and from the Conservative Party has tacitly acknowledged inefficiencies of this nature by putting exceptional emphasis on the need for initiative, energy, and responsibility.

The system of economic individualism is not sufficiently zealous about treating workers as men. There is still virtue in the phrase in the Treaty of Versailles, Part XIII, which established the International Labor Office, that "Labor is not

[26] Pp. 47-49 T.N.E.C. Monograph, Dimock, *Bureaucracy and Trusteeship in Large Corporations.*

a commodity," that is, that it ought not to be treated simply as a commodity. It has required many decades of the most resolute action to make sure that the employers put safety devices into their factories. It requires constant pressure to secure their administration and the inspectorial effect. It even requires international conventions to secure these things, and even here, when solemn engagements have been undertaken, there is constant complaint that they are not executed fully. It has taken decades of political contest to bring about proper laws for the payment of compensation to workers suffering from occupational accidents and disease, and they have been fought by employers, who were thereby endeavoring to throw part of their proper expenses of production on others. Until the United States Supreme Court reacted to the election returns, economic individualism would not admit the reasonableness of employers' liability. Yet, steadily, the accidents go on. In British industry there are 400,000 disablements per year, and some 2500 are killed, and in the United States some 2,000,000 disablements and 18,000 deaths per year.

Even if, which is doubtful, there were always efficiency in the relationship between any two enterprisers for the meeting of and paying business risks by insurance, as the risks relate to them, there is still the problem of the damage done to the public at large. For example, it is a regular complaint by property owners that they are expected to provide protection against fire, or the collapse of their buildings. They meet their own troubles, and, let us say, the troubles of those who lodge their goods in their warehouses, by insurance; but collapse of buildings, fire, and so on affect other parties altogether — innocent wayfarers, or neighbors. Hayek is now prepared to condone factory and building regulations, without realizing that his immaculate businessmen have to be forced into proper ways.

Competition has had little interest in the conservation of

resources. It is an exploiter, and conducts what the Germans have called *Raubwirtschaft* — a robber economy, or an economy of prey. Forests have been cut down without rational replanting; land which was protected from erosion by standing timber has been ruined; plowing for cash crops has been undertaken without any concern for the destruction of the land, which has not been nourished by irrigation and fertilizer.[27] Coal reserves[28] have been exploited and utilized in the most profligate manner. Oil and gas have been similarly wasted to make purely private fortunes at private discretion.

## 6. *Mass Unemployment*

Competition is unable to find employment for all its willing workers all the time. There is always some unemployment, but mass unemployment, with its consequent loss of national wealth, and the misery of the individual workers and their families, is not to be condoned. The figures of distress have been given on Pages 157 ff. above.

It is not the present object to pursue into all its detail the distress produced by unemployment. The chief cause of disquiet, apart from the decrease in the potential wealth of the nations, is misery of mind and desperation in the person unemployed, because neither he nor his family is secure, and therefore he is haunted by fear. Such evils breed detestation of orderly government, hatred of employers, and hatred of man for man, for any man, and especially for a man of a different race who may take the bread out of the mouth of one's family. It ought to be pointed out in regard to Great Britain, which is the country about which *The Road to Serfdom* was first written, that in each year between the two wars three out of every ten working people, and in a bad year five out of every ten, experienced some unem-

[27] Cf. *Recent Social Trends,* I, pp. 93ff.
[28] *Ibid.*, pp. 85ff.

ployment while, between July 1924 and December 1932, two out of every three working people of all ages made a claim to unemployment benefit. It is no surprise to find that in such circumstances the workers organize to defend their interest and, when they have the power, to insist on restrictions of output and technical improvement. In the United States similar fears of unemployment produced the same consequences in defensive restrictiveness, and assisted the movement toward race discrimination.

The inter-war depression was particularly violent as far as we can now tell because of the special effects of World War I, but for decades the recurrence of depressions has been noticed, and the misery and fears of the workers which followed suggested to Karl Marx that catastrophe would come to the state on one of these occasions. But consider Mr. Lippmann, who has always been so reasonable about morals and government. I do not know whether when he wrote *The Good Society* in 1936–1937 he took a private bet that he could write a book so entitled without a single mention of the word "unemployment." The subject would then have certainly been relevant, for in 1936 there were still six and a half million unemployed, and in 1937, seven and a half million; and there was a distinctly rising trend. The plague had been on for seven years. Yet it is a fact that not once in four hundred pages does the word or the idea of unemployment appear! It is difficult to understand how the Introduction to the 1943 Edition can claim, as it does, that "the experience through which we have passed since the book was first published has not shaken, but has, in fact, strengthened my conviction that it contains more truth than error." But its remedies for the sickness of a competitive society did not concern themselves with unemployment. Perhaps, though I do not think so, he shares the opinion ventured in 1931 by Albert H. Wiggin of the Chase National Bank, to a Senate Committee on a National Economic Council:

"Human nature is human nature. Lives go on. So long as business activity goes on we are bound to have conditions of crisis once in so often." When Senator La Follette prompted, "The capacity for human suffering is unlimited?" Mr. Wiggin replied: "I think so," and submitted a one-page summary of the doctrine of the market, of prices, and *laissez faire!*

The root cause of this mass unemployment — or to put it another way, of depressions — has been the subject of much difference between economists for many years. But the explanation now put forward by Sir William Beveridge in the English tradition, founded on the discoveries in economic theory of J. M. Keynes, also in the English tradition, is generally accepted. It is that depression is due to instability of business investment. All the national income is accounted for in two ways: some is spent on current consumption, the rest returns into investment for the production of capital equipment like factories, factory equipment, houses, raw materials, warehouses, and so on. There is some steadiness about consumption. There is none about investment, though there is no unsteadiness of any note about the human need for productive equipment. To what, then, is the instability of investment due? It is due to the fact that decisions to save, and decisions to invest, are made by different people at different times, for different reasons.

Sir William Beveridge, who has given what must now be more than two thirds of his life to the study of the phenomenon of unemployment, is convinced that mass unemployment can be abolished. He believes it can be held down to about 3 per cent, which is the figure caused by seasonal fluctuations and the necessary changes of men from one occupation to another, as technological change and changes in demand cause some trades to decline while others are growing. He believes that this can be done *in a free society;* that is his basic condition, and he demonstrates

ence on "the important question whether those who rely on the community should indefinitely enjoy all the same liberties as the rest"! (Page 120.) This kind of thing was deliberately tried in Great Britain in bygone ages, on the recommendation of the classical economists, in the poor law system instituted in 1835. This is the system that Hayek likes. Speaking at Harvard University he mentioned his principle of relief, that is, "outside the competitive system," and "to cope with extreme physical privation." He then supported his argument by a quotation from the economist William Nassau Senior, but without dwelling on Senior's real purpose until the present author challenged the quotation. Only then did Hayek admit that Senior's views had called for principles of relief that were "less eligible" than those of the poorest independent worker, that relief was to be "deterrent," and that the test of whether it was needed was to be that it would be given only if the applicant for relief took it *in the Poorhouse.*

This system was tried in all its original crudity for about two decades, but it was impossible to maintain it against the protests of the workers and those who said that the economic system was to blame, not the individual. In fact (though Hayek did not continue his excursion into economic history) the moral untenability of the system, and the waste economically, eventually started a whole host of social investigations into the problem of unemployment. The two most vigorous and creative workers were Sidney and Beatrice Webb, and their efforts led in the end to the establishment of public employment exchanges, and a social insurance system. It was they who kindled in Sir William Beveridge an interest in problems of unemployment, and they introduced him to Mr. Winston Churchill, to see him become under the latter at the Home Office the first organizer of these same employment exchanges. It was as a result of their analyses of exactly how the labor market does function, and

conclusively how it can be done. He is in the English tradition, and cares for freedom at least as much as Hayek alleges that he does. A man of vast and important administrative experience, he certainly understands the political and administrative significance and secrets of freedom. Furthermore, he has demonstrated the necessity and the method of providing social security, or the maintenance of income, during the contingencies of unemployment, even at a rate of 8 per cent, and for the other contingencies, like maternity, old age, invalidity, occupational disease and accident, and so on.

His scheme involves far-reaching state direction of investment. Its main features can only be listed: they are social security and children's allowances; collective outlay for good houses, food, fuel and other necessaries at stable prices for all, and free national health service; a national investment board to encourage and regulate private investment, to review and expand the mechanical equipment of the nation, in stable progress; control of monopolies by nationalizing, if necessary, and extending public industry in order directly to stabilize investment; control of location of industry and transport; organized mobility of labor; controlled marketing of primary products; international trading arrangements; a budget to ensure full demand for all use of all productive resources.

The United States has the same problem. In both countries the problem is aggravated by the fact that during World War II, and certainly as a result of the very bitter experience during the great depression, men and women have come to demand security as a first charge on the national productive machine. They are prepared, indeed, anxious to work: but they insist that there must be work. Hence, the current demand for the general principle of 60,000,000 jobs. Sir William Beveridge's general principles are being adapted to the American scene. Their essential character is that there shall always be more jobs vacant than there are men wanting them, and not the reverse.

What is the attitude of the reactionaries to this problem? *The Road to Serfdom* declares it plainly. The maintenance of economic individualism and the Engineer's Clock is more important than employment. "In a competitive society it is no slight to a person, no offense to his dignity, to be told by any particular firm that it has no need for his services or that it cannot offer him a better job. It is true that in periods of prolonged mass unemployment the effect on many may be very similar.[29] But there are other and better methods to prevent that scourge than central direction." (Page 106.)

Does he then exert himself to say what these methods are? It would have been worth the whole of *The Road to Serfdom* if he could have offered a convincing description of *The Road to Employment*. He prefers not to do this.

He says: "There is, finally, the supremely important problem of combating general fluctuations of economic activity and the recurrent waves of large-scale unemployment which accompany them. This is, of course, one of the gravest and most pressing problems of our time. But, though its solution will require much planning in the good sense [he must mean *for* competition!] it does not — or at least need not — require that special kind of planning which according to its advocates is to replace the market." He refers to the hope that it may be done by "monetary policy" — and we are left unilluminated whether he means taxation or investment strategy. Others, he mentions, believe that real success can be expected only from the skillful timing of public works undertaken on a very large scale. Here Hayek is a little frightened lest the result be to make "all economic activity

[29] See Walter Greenwood, *Love on the Dole;* George Orwell, *The Road to Wigan Pier;* Bakke, *The Unemployed Worker;* Ginzberg, *Grass on the Slagheaps.*

progressively more dependent on the direction and volume of government expenditure." (Page 121 and Page 122.)

The only other contribution to this problem, the warning that no "single purpose must be allowed in peace to have absolute preference over all others," applies "even to the one aim which everybody now agrees comes in the front rank: the conquest of unemployment." (Page 206.) He warns that "vague but popular phrases like 'full employment' may well lead to extremely shortsighted measures"; and he tells us that the reallocation of war workers to the peacetime pattern of production should not be obstructed by the attempt to maintain the jobs and the relative wartime scales of pay. What a husk! He cannot forthrightly say that competition can do the job of finding the jobs. It is the system at all costs.

With fastidious responsibility to competition and the Engineer's Clock, Hayek observes that no man has a right to any particular job at a given pay. But he is willing to give "*security against severe physical privation,* the certainty of a given minimum of sustenance for all." (Page 120.) That is, to *give* it: not to make it an insurable proposition. What is the standard to be? "There can be no doubt that some minimum of food, shelter, and clothing, sufficient to preserve health and the capacity to work, can be assured to everybody." Great Britain is wealthy enough to provide this without endangering the general freedom, he says. Notice the caution with which the standard is stated: "severe physical privation," and "sufficient to preserve health and the capacity to work." Would this apply even with mass unemployment, in which, for all his designation of it as the most serious problem, such a lukewarm interest is betrayed?

We must add his observation, which is consonant with his whole attitude, that this security for all is outside of and supplementary to the market system. That is, it is a kind of charity or poor law. This idea is reinforced by his insist-

the causes of unemployment and destitution, that the poor law, as such, was broken up into a number of more helpful social services and social insurance. Ultimately, by Sir William Beveridge's Report and by later legislation, the system of social insurance was given a comprehensiveness and a principle which it had hitherto lacked. The leading ideas convinced American economists and social scientists.

Now the Webbs inveighed against the great error of treating destitution on the basis of what they called "physical destitution." Sir William Beveridge also argues that men should have a "subsistence" wage — he takes the subsistence standard as deduced from the cost of living. In his plans for employment, Sir William lays it down that "We need . . . that each man and woman shall be assured of an income for honourable subsistence and maintenance of any dependents, when for any reason, he or she is unable to work."

In the case of sickness and calamity Hayek is prepared to see the state assist in the provision of insurance (Page 121), but he is not prepared to see the state make a system of insurance compulsory.[30] Yet it has been clearly demonstrated that social insurance can only be managed adequately and economically if it is universal; and if it is universal it requires that all shall enter in by authority.

## 7. Despoliation of Other Economic Enterprisers

It is impossible in the compass of the present essay to survey, even briefly, and certainly with the rich picturesqueness they deserve, the predatory practices of business, especially big business in the course of its rise since the Civil War. Yet the subject is important because it vitally affects two of the theses set out by Hayek and lapped up by his friends of today: that is, his bland assumption that there is

[30] Radio Discussion, Round Table, Chicago.

no coercion in competition, and that in dictatorships the worst get to the top because planning requires coercion. I therefore merely list some of the practices which the famous congressional investigations have absolutely authenticated, supplemented by the findings at criminal and equity trials in the law courts. I always hope that I will arrive at some terminal point where I can say, "After all, that is the history of a ruder age." In fact, no sooner do I do this, than some other scandal breaks, and the same old tricks are once more reported by Congress and the courts. Here is the list of monopolistic and competitive tactics: menaces and intrigues; use of armed guards and thugs against competitors and their employees; destruction at night of property of rivals; secret rebates on railways; buying up of newspapers and journalists; bribery; secret commissions; spying and intimidation of other firms; plain dishonesty to all parties to a transaction; dilatory litigation; extensive conspiracies; the killing off of competition where the rival is small enough; the exploitation of easy-virtue charters of incorporation; demoralization of judges, juries, legislators and officials; watering, manipulation and false boosting of stocks and bonds; driving rivals into bankruptcy; maneuvers for managerial sovereignty over many adjacent sectors of finance and industry; secret agreements; plain swindling; repudiation of contracts; debauching the future by heated installment selling; deception of the public by the spread of false news; price discrimination (one of the more recent methods is the Pittsburgh-plus system); false advertising; misbranding; defamation of competitors; "tying" contracts; fighting brands; exclusive dealer system. And the lawbooks are full of cases concerning cheating with trade marks, by confusing similarity, plain appropriation, repackaging and reprocessing and refilling original containers; adulteration of food and drugs; inducing breach of contract. We may add, when on the witness stand before Congress or the Courts, the failure of memory and ignorance of crucial detail. There is a very large literature on this subject. Why is it forgotten?

All these evils have been kept in rein only by the strongest exertion of the state in the democratic countries, because hitherto the economically powerful have been able to commandeer the state. These evils are deep-seated and persistent. Both Hayek and Lippmann express their sense of betrayal that the "liberals," that is the *laissez faire* advocates of the nineteenth and twentieth centuries, behaved as badly as they did in so capturing industry and defying the demands for political remedy. But the "liberal" could not be what they would have wished him to be: when he said *laissez faire,* he really meant *laissez faire.* He was interested in what went in his pocket, not what went on in Hayek's mind. His dismay that the men to whom he lends perfection are unmitigated egoists, endangering by their avarice the state which guarantees property and freedom, is the dismay of the cuckold.

A clear proof of Hayek's inability to understand the phenomena outside his window is his pathetic remark: "One thing that makes me unhappy is that so many people who take up my book are not free-traders and do not see that this is an essential part of the same philosophy." [81]

They certainly see that it is an essential part of the same philosophy. But where they differ from Hayek is that while he wants competition they want freedom and money.

A supplement and a direction are required if even any substantial part of the competitive system is to be allowed to remain. It is silly to resist the necessary changes which may keep it, insofar as it is valuable, alive. But this is what Hayek does.

[81] *University of Chicago Round Table No. 370,* p. 5.

## CHAPTER X

# The Most Splendid Race

There is only one cure for the evils which newly acquired freedom produces; and that cure is freedom.

— MACAULAY

The reactionary Manifesto makes no case in support of the successful stockbroker, manufacturer, or merchant who kills and eats his unsuccessful rival, although this cannibalism would seem to be the proper logical consequence of triumph in the practice of competition. Whatever moderation there is in Hayek springs from the recognition that there is, and ought to be, a law above the results of economic competition, that there ought to be some constraint based on decency. There is, in other words, an acknowledgment that socially accepted and imposed moral standards, noneconomic moral standards, shall hold in leash the economic process. The real question that remains to be answered, then, is not whether or not we shall move at all, but how far, and for what advantages and against what disadvantages.

Government is the conduct of the affairs of a *society* so that, it being necessary that there shall be choices of values and a doctrine of destiny, there be some power above all the many individuals and the many thousands of groupings in that society. This power is a medium through which the moral and physical force of the groups or group predominant at any one time shall prevail. In a democracy the balance of these forces is always shifting and contingent, not fixed and ordained: ample provision is made for the almost daily adjustment of the justice, spirituality, grossness, economic power, and physical force by which people commend themselves to others. Religion finds its due place herein: and so properly does the business of getting and spending an income. Locke's terse summary suffices: —

> God, having made man such a creature that, in His own judgment, it was not good for him to be alone, put him under strong obligations of necessity, convenience and inclination, to drive him into society, as well as fitted him with understanding and language to continue and enjoy it. . . . And thus all private judgment of every particular member being excluded, the community comes to be umpire by settled standing rules, indifferent and the same to all parties; . . . decides all the differences that may happen between any members of that society concerning any matter of right. . . .

The issue before us is not freedom in general, nor freedom outside democracy. The issue is freedom in particular, as related to specific objects of democracy's claims on the individual. There have always been two phases of the struggle for freedom or liberty at every moment in history: the larger phase of the location of rightful authority, and, within that, and partly as its fulfillment in practice, the degrees of liberty and authority in the solution of any particular question.

These two problems are implicit in the generalized policy outlined below, and much of the time that democracies spend in considering such a policy is devoted to their consideration. The time it takes to carry out such a policy is determined by the good sense of the majority, working with that reciprocity and mutuality of tolerance which is the balancing spirit of democracy.

The policy is: —

Full employment and a rising standard of living.

Social security.

Social services, especially health and education and housing.

Open access to jobs.

Direct public ownership and management of the utilities of transport, communications, water, gas, electricity, fuel if they fail to respond to public standards, by existing and improved methods of regulation.

Equalizing measures, as in the taxation of inheritances.

Encouragement of the return to personal ownership of agricultural land, on the condition of the co-operative agriculture required by modern technology and respondent to the nutrition policy of the country founded on modern science; continuance and amplification of the services rendered by the Department of Agriculture in soil conservation, seed experimenting, fertilizer experimenting, and the services of guidance, education, health, domestic economy, as under the Farm Security Administration.

The organization, mobilization and financing of invention.

Clearing of the road for competition in the fields where it is untouched by public enterprise is suggested here. Expanding the R.F.C. and letting it be more adventurous.

Control over the location of industries.

Public enterprise along both conservationist and exploitative lines.

Much is already being done with a slightly different emphasis and scope in each of these fields in the United States and Great Britain. There is a tremendous amount of acquired experience, and a remarkable body of knowledge and tradition and "know-how" in the service of the two nations.

The establishment of a public medical service, one of the subjects which are now on the agenda of the United States and Great Britain, will serve as an illustration of a way in which these subjects can be approached. It is advocated that this service be transferred to state initiative, because the purchase of medical assistance from individual doctors by individuals through fees does not provide that attention to the health of all which is now regarded by a substantial majority of society as being moral. It has taken a long time to come to this. One hundred years ago it was even contended by some people that to establish isolation hospitals for the control of contagious disease, and to require the removal of garbage alleged to cause disease, were improper interference with the designs of Providence, and that when people were afflicted with disease it was a matter between them and God, who had his inscrutable but unimpugnable intentions. And in 1848 Herbert Spencer argued that the state ought not to license physicians or forbid unlicensed quacks to prescribe: to do so "is directly to violate the moral law"! Spencer goes on in Hayek's unmistakable voice: "The invalid is at liberty to buy medicine from whomsoever he pleases; the unlicensed practitioner is at liberty to sell to whomsoever will buy"! Society does not now intend to remain at the point of the environmental services of sewerage, clean water, clean streets, the collection of garbage, the abatement of smoke, the putting down of dust, and curative action after sickness has set in. There now prevails the conception that it is possible to fortify the human body against the common ailments, and many that are not so common but which will yield to treatment and care. The prevention of ill-health has been accepted as a public policy. Incidentally, this policy has been proved to be economically profitable, because it avoids the expenditure of money on remedies and keeps people strong enough to avoid loss of work.[1] Now what is to be done with an idea of this kind? To give its benefits to some and not to others affronts democracy, where it is felt that all have an equal right to life and health and care for their family. If incomes are unequal how can general health be attained except by the social assumption of responsibilities for universal medical service?

Here is an actual issue of planning: the provision of an economic service which hitherto has been subject to the rule of prices and the market. We are informed that of all causes of happiness physical well-being is near the top of the list. Assume that the sovereign people decide that a state medical service shall be put into practice, the next thing is how it can be done (a) at the least expense so that all shall have as much as possible of the rest of their money in order to buy other things; (b) so that the best possible medical service shall be rendered, and (c) that people shall be free to get the service, which not only is objectively best, but which they *feel* to be best, and (d) that the medical profession shall not feel unfree under the responsibilities they are to exercise in the service of the public authority.

I can name no less than twenty different methods of answering each of these problems, and each varies the devices and degrees in which the methods are utilized. There is one answer in New Zealand; and another in Australia; still another in Sweden, and a fourth in England. In the discussions now proceeding in England, there is the most careful weighing of the following factors: Should private prac-

[1] *Cf. Political and Economic Planning, The British Health Services,* 1937. One fifteenth of the entire British income was spent on ill-health, chiefly as remedies.

tice continue under a national medical care service, or should there be no private practice, or some? How can the free choice of doctor be arranged for, to preserve the confidential healing relationship between doctor and patient — and how arrange for continuity of care? What will be the status of the doctor? How will he be appointed, how disciplined — by his own professional body or by whom? And what will be the character of supervision by the state — will this be by the local authority as now constituted, or by a different kind of local authority? Will remuneration be by salary or by a fee per person attended? What working conditions will be established, and by what authority? How will the cost be distributed, by special tax or general tax or by insurance payment? What will be the form of democratic control, and what arrangements ought to be made for the rights of complaint and appeal?

The variety of devices for securing a feasible balance of service and liberty is literally legion. We do not have to be either anarchically a nation of which one third is in ill-health; nor need we become a nation bursting with health but at the same time bursting with revolutionary resentment against a body of state doctors manhandling and physicking us for our good that we do not want, as Hayek would caricature it.

And, as it is with the health services, so it is with almost any economic service that can be named. What, for example, is unfree or slavish about a scientific nutrition policy and an international agreement, like the Food and Agriculture Commission, to induce nations to produce according to an agreed plan? There was, by the way, at one time an outcry against the state's giving free and compulsory education.

The question is how to inch along in the democratic way, so that we may never lose our basic treasure, which is democracy — that is, the power to move forwards and backwards *at will*. This involves five pillars of democracy which need some discussion, but in this context only at certain crucial points. They are: (1) Majority Rule; (2) Parties and the Press; (3) Reform of the Legislature; (4) Reform of the Executive; (5) Public Services.

## 1. *Majority Rule*

Every member of a democratic society with voting rights is a sovereign ruler of his country. His responsibility, whether he knows it or not, is a tremendous one. His principal duty is to make his choices in such a way that the possibility of reversing the laws he wishes to be enacted is always open. The laws of planning must not be such, directly or indirectly, as to subtract from the sufficient guarantee of periodic elections, with public opinion freely expressible, the instruments thereof untrammeled, associations for electoral purposes not inhibited, and the executive as well as the legislature of the state dependent on the outcome of these elections. This is the prime stabilizing rule for the majority. This will give them the guarantee of freedom, in whatever way they like to define freedom. Freedom is sometimes differentiated from liberty, it being said that freedom is no government or control whatsoever, while liberty is that freedom which is permitted by the laws democratically made. I prefer the plain definition of freedom in psychological terms, as "the possibility of continuous initiative." This cannot be exercised completely in respect to everything in any state man has known, once out of the mythological state of nature. But we need it in as many fields as possible, and there is no possibility of "continuous initiative" open to persons without an income.

In order that there may be available to the majority a basis for choice among alternatives, it must continue and deepen its education. Immersion in the history of systems of government has been badly neglected: this would reveal the essential principles of the democratic system, that it is an instrument to be *used* for social and individual ends, tolerance to other views and the keeping open of the door of government to any newly formed majority. Above all it must learn the profundities of Montesquieu's injunction regarding the spirit in which a democracy must be conducted: "There is no great share of probity," he says, "necessary to support a monarchical or despotic government. The force of the laws in one, and the prince's arm in the other, are sufficient to direct and maintain the whole. But in a popular state, one spring more is necessary, namely, *virtue*. . . . Virtue is a self-renunciation, which is ever arduous and painful." And he, like all the noble spirits who have wished that humanity should become increasingly master of itself and not the slave of either political or economic bosses, asserts that "it is in a republican government that the whole power of education is required," so that we may learn a constant preference of public to private interest.

The second need of the majority is to acquire a much deeper understanding of the economic process through theory and economic history, political science, public administration, and the other social sciences. The more people learn these things, the greater the basis among them of social agreement. But those who do not want the education need not have it, just as those who do not want to vote need not. An extraordinary proportion of the people do vote.

The majority will not be oppressive to large minorities. It has the right to move ahead when the minority is small. It will never have a need to be cruel. It is minorities, rather, which arrogate to themselves these privileges. But it must be remembered that a majority does not arrive out of the clouds. The people must be approached to make a majority, and persuaded to join in the majority. While there is free discussion and the organization of parties is continuous and alive, demagogues cannot gain a majority.

Those who work at any occupation acquire, by the age of twenty-five, especially if they are married and beginning to found a family, some stable good sense which is what we must rely on. At any rate there is no other form of government which guarantees freedom in the long run as majority rule does. Since it has tolerated the institutional procedures for self-control and for the deliberate consideration of governmental measures, we may have a sober confidence that it will continue to develop freedom. We do not need to fall into the thoroughly Hitlerian contempt for the democratic man so perfectly expressed by Hayek: "Probably it is true enough that the great majority are rarely capable of thinking independently, that on most questions they accept views which they find ready-made, and that they will be equally content if born or coaxed into one set of beliefs or another. In any society freedom of thought will probably be of direct significance only for a small minority." (Page 164.) And this man has the audacity or opaqueness to charge that "Englishmen who not only 'the language speak that Shakespeare spoke' but also 'the faith and morals hold that Milton held' seem to have almost vanished" leaving only Hayek!

## 2. Parties and the Press

In both the United States and Great Britain democratic government is party government, that is, the electorate has organized itself and is organized to follow certain leaders and principles. The parties are not authoritarian impositions on the people, but emanations of the people. As democracy has been worked for not many decades in geographically wide and socially complex societies, the people have not yet altogether realized that they ought to enter into the operations of their parties at the earliest instance. Membership is open to them, and they can participate in the two fundamental functions of the party: first, the establishment of its program for the government of the country, comprising what laws ought to be passed, what their internal nature should be and how they should be administered, and what money has to be found to meet the cost; and second, the selection of candidates for the legislature. The whole task requires more rational procedures. We know that all group life has certain oligarchic tendencies, but there is nothing wrong with that, provided the way is wide open for challenging the actions and existence of the oligarchy. Democracy means the distribution of leadership for more virile activity, not for passivity: that was its justification. It is in political parties and other associations that the individual in modern society can find the truly strategic opportunity for choice of the kind of life he would like to live, for thinking and challenging thought and so helping to develop it, and for indulgence in that planning of his own destiny which Hayek says is the essential of freedom. It is more open to people to have a say in the conduct of government by participating in the party organization than it is for the gainfully occupied population to have a share in the control of the economy.

It is from in and around the life of the parties and the contiguous and competing associations that the steady stimulus comes to state enterprise: to do or not to do; to make, supply, and deliver in such and such quantities the goods and services of various kinds. Not in all detail, for there are other well-known "market techniques" and "market research" developed by public administration no less than by private business, which can be the monitor of state-directed production and distribution. The idea that in a planned economy there would be no consumer's choice is one more of those suggestions which are refutable by the merest tyro in economic theory, and which Hayek could not have made inadvertently.

The press has a vital part to play. It is to be wondered

whether those who control or write for it universally realize the magnitude of their responsibility. The press is private property exercising one of the most vital public services to a democracy, and capable, because it is private property, of a perversion of the function of news reporting and editorial comment. Every newspaper has some tale about the misdemeanors of another newspaper, and a severe one at that; all the press together rightly is the defender of freedom, but it sometimes condones license. There are members of the press who are not interested in everybody's obtaining the news for public dissemination.[2] There is only one way of permanently maintaining the freedom of the press — fairness to all parties; not neutrality, but not falsification of information, exaggeration of attitudes, use of logical fallacies, ignorance, neglect of the true perspective of history. Rather the same holds good of the radio, and particularly of the commentators, who in so many cases are ignorant of history, crassly uninformed about other nations, strange to diplomatic records, innocent of economic theory and development and of parliamentary procedure, and afflicted with the belief that to be interesting they must offer scandals and sensations. The record of some in the matter of inter-Allied relations is a betrayal of trust to the public. Even so, American freedom of discussion on the air is superior to British public corporation control. The latter has so far not realized its potentialities because, concerned for flat impartiality, it is difficult for listeners to realize that there are two sides to the matter, or any matter at all. It is my hope that something can be done to preserve that independence which allows the presentation of strong views on the American radio, and that sense of public service which excludes from the scarce air time pontiffs with an entire want of preparation for the role they dare to assume. So long as there is the opportunity of immediate

[2] *Cf. U. S.* v. *Associated Press* (June 1945).

and intense rebuttal, I would give the rein to the fiercest affirmation.

## 3. Reform of the Legislature

The legislature is the heart of the planning process, for it is here that the less authoritative and less definite programs of the parties enter for definition and authorization. The size of the legislature should be increased to about 750. The purpose of the increase is twofold: to decrease the size of congressional districts and so bring the people closer to the representatives, which would be an inducement to enter into the inner life of the party caucus; and to provide an adequate number of persons for legislative committees which will be needed to study and report upon legislation in its preparatory stages. Much good work is already done in this respect: it could be improved by the employment of able professional assistants, and if the legislature abated its jealousy of the executive, there might be a permanent, organized liaison between the legislative committees and the departments. These committees would play a very important part in investigating the operations of the executive, whether in the form of the routine departments, or independent, regulatory commissions, or in the form of public corporations; they therefore need to be rationally organized as regards number, size, composition, times of session, and procedure.

Politics is no game: it is the serious management of the great society and the great economy. The rationalization of the legislature is an urgent duty. Of special importance among the tasks of the committees in control of the executive is the surveillance of the so-called "delegated legislation" which the executive is deputed to make to fulfill the laws enacting the main principle. It should, however, not be believed that the House of Representatives and the

House of Commons make their enactments only in outline. On the contrary, they go into the most considerable detail. There has been much thought on this by the courts of law in recent years, and their suggestions regarding the proper laying down of definite standards of legislation have been applied.

It is of the highest importance to draft the laws with precision. A law is one stage between the will of the people and the eventual behavior of the people implemented by the public officials who are given the laws to administer. If it is precise, it is a service done to the people, and there will be no recriminations about legislative usurpation. If it is precise, again, there can be no charge of "bureaucracy," and one of the supreme services will have been rendered to the public officers themselves: they will know their limits of endeavor and enterprise.

From the time of Alexander Hamilton's famous report on manufactures of December 5, 1791, the legislatures and the executives have established their policy on the basis of careful, previous investigations. These instrumental inquiries should be increased in number and scope and improved in method.

## 4. *Reform of the Executive*

I am confident that the United States of the twentieth century cannot be adequately served with the one-man Presidency. The responsibility put upon one man is far too heavy. The purposes of the Founding Fathers in establishing this unit responsibility was to obtain vigor and dispatch, and concentration of responsibility where it would be unmistakable. One-man executive responsibility can no longer accomplish these things if it ever did — for one man cannot make up his mind without many advisers, and the responsibility is so paralyzing as to invite delay, evasion, and an unwillingness to devolve responsibility and power to assistants, for the mistakes made by any assistant may properly be visited upon the President. It is necessary to have a cabinet with collective responsibility. Real collective responsibility requires the ability to rely on other people and their right to intervene in the affairs of any other department at the formative stage if it appears that a mistake is about to be perpetrated. Also the knowledge that others have concurred is a weight off the shoulders of the one taking the initiative, and therefore it encourages initiative.

This, however, can only be properly accomplished if some permanent and productive formal liaison between the White House and the Congress is discovered.

Without such a collective cabinet the business of securing executive integration is well-nigh impossible. Attempts have been made to achieve this by the reorganization of the departments and their relationship with each other. This has not proved very satisfactory, because there is still only one man with real responsibility. Together with the reform of the executive, it is essential to intermesh the budget and investigatory devices for securing the responsibility of the various administrative departments. Co-ordination, so necessary as the state takes on more functions, is not a mere product of executive gadgetry, but the product of a legislature intimately allied with the chief executive (the Cabinet) and with a power of damnation in its hands. The voices of the legislators can be raised early and often enough to discipline the executive and its officials. Cabinet members must be brought back to the floor of Congress where their faces can be seen: for the faces will not lie, not on two successive days, or at any rate, not on three. Detection is the product of physical proximity. The future of the state does not depend on men being virtuous without criticism and discipline. Not that Cabinet members are bad — that question does not arise — but they may do too little or too much or not the things that the legislators want done.

Much thought has been spent on this subject, and many brains have been at work. All have a multitude of good proposals. The chief concern of all is to get the executive and the legislative into a practically seamless connection. They must not be aliens to each other.

## 5. *Public Services*

This is usually where the antiplanner begins to sneer. But the sneer has no more public value than those sneers and designations which competitive businessmen utter about each other's business methods unless there is a joint profit to be had. Most of these calumnies are as unfounded in fact as the "false and fraudulent disparagement" in business of which American and English law courts have been obliged to take notice. The critic of "bureaucracy" has not taken the trouble to reflect upon the remarkable inventions and the self-control of democracy in setting up the merit system of appointment based on open competition — that is, the career open to talent without favor of family fortune and influence. In perspective, it is a grand achievement. Every day new ideas are being produced by a half-million public servants at a salary. Those who have not seen the literature on the subject are missing a view of one of mankind's supreme efforts of invention. It is on a par, indeed, with that which occurred a century and a half ago, when, as Hayek said or Adam Smith said before him, the division or specialization of labor was "tumbled upon." This new enormously complicated yet integrated and dynamic organization is as complex as the brain of man can comprehend, but it responds to certain simple principles of organization, and it works with fertility in the public cause.

A civil servant or a public employee is nothing other than

a businessman in the service of public affairs. The problem of recruitment has been solved, with the exception that we are still at a loss about character elements. That is a problem which arises in business too. Business gets rid of its mistakes, though by no means with the celerity alleged. The more fully planned states will have to do this also. It is not recruitment, but ejection of deadwood which is the public service's *pons asinorum* — making a bridge for the donkeys to take on their swift way home.

The subject usually raised by the planner is the want of incentive in the planned state. "Who gets what, when and how?" as Hayek quotes Lasswell. The ordinary run of men and women, however, want security of income. They cannot and do not expect fortunes. Only a few people have an overweening belief that they could make millions, and not so many wish to put in the effort to try. They will be paid in the service of the state as they are paid in the service of any employer, and that is their inducement to work at that job. We do not have to rely upon any exceptional sense of public service. People work for a living, and security is a vital consideration. They may be disciplined for not doing their work. They may be subject to stated fines. There would be less difference in the comparative advantages of the different jobs, that is, the money income and the hours, holidays, agreeableness of the work, and the like, taken together, than in present society, for gradually inequality of fortunes and education would be lifted, and each person would be on a higher level of attainment and freedom to choose which complex of advantages and disadvantages best suited him personally. It is ridiculous to believe, as Hayek affects to believe, that the problems of recruitment and remuneration are insoluble.

What about the incentive of the great fortune makers — the "captains of industry"? Those days, when luck and first-there gave enormous fortunes, are going; the great monopolies show that. The state can search for inventions as well as any independent, economic entrepreneur. Inventors are born. They do not need the kind of encouragement a captain of industry needs. The question really is the commercial exploitation of an invention.

The public in a planned state would demand goods and services of as many varieties as it does today. It would have just as much interest in abundance and change, and would express that interest to the managers of the state stores. Municipal planning of gas, water, and electricity supply was advocated in England by small and big business because government officials could be trusted better than their fellow businessmen to provide the services dependably, without discrimination between consumers, and at a lower cost of production. Secondly, there would be a focus of social demand in the legislatures and in the public services themselves, and they could be expected to continue to propose such vast enterprises as the Birmingham (England) gas department which operates the largest and most inventive artificial gas plant in the world, and such large projects as the Tennessee Valley Authority and other hydroelectric schemes, and the Maritime Commission, and the Reconstruction Finance Corporation.

It is not helpful to parade an ignorance of such projects, as Hayek does; nor ignorance of the fact that British cities, in their administration of the public utilities, have shown easily as much inventive interest as any big business — in improvement, in the scrapping of old capital, in the discovery of new resources, in the arrangement of techniques of stimulation and loyalty, and checks and balances, and verification of efficiency.[3] If those who are fearful of "public-businessmen" wish to appreciate how highly enterprising and efficient they may be, they need not contemplate the minor

[3] *Cf.* Finer, *Municipal Enterprise* (London, 1941).

218

clerical officers in government but rather the great city managers.

There is in the nation a vast and yet untapped reservoir of human energy and ability which can operate such enterprises, and which will one day astound the world, and shame it that it was so long neglected. Splendid talent is begging for an opportunity. It cannot find it in private business leadership, because in many cases private enterprise has not the capital, or the courage, or the brains, and in many cases talent will not stoop to those methods of private enterprise falsely believed to be necessary to the rendering of the service in question. The United States and Great Britain have cause to be proud of great victories in civil administration.

For hundreds of years society was without this class of public servants, and state administration limped. The greatest inventions of the nineteenth and the twentieth centuries have not been physical inventions, great as they have been. The two greatest inventions of the nineteenth century are representative and responsible democracy, and expert and impartial public administration. Public administration, besides the personnel, consists of three things to which attention is being given night and day by hundreds of anxious minds: the federal–state relationship, retaining the advantages of local thought and local application of measures; the written and personal liaison between the center and the extremities; and the securing of the responsibility of the official for the due fulfillment of the plan of democracy, as stated in the law. The checks internal to the administration are themselves almost a substitute for the old-fashioned separation of powers.

No mistake could be greater than that of Hayek (Page 20) to the effect that interest in planning society has come from habits of thought promoted by natural science and engineering. But long before our society was influenced by technology there were men — Plato and Aristotle and Christ may be recalled — who were interested in societies not being unprincipled. In 1776, the year of the Declaration of Independence and *Wealth of Nations,* Jeremy Bentham opened his *Fragment on Government* with this paragraph: —

The age we live in is a busy age; an age in which knowledge is rapidly advancing towards perfection. In the natural world, in particular, everything teems with discovery and with improvement. . . . Correspondent to discovery and improvement in the natural world, is reformation in the moral . . . perhaps among such observations as would be best calculated to serve as grounds for reformation are some which, being observations of matters of fact hitherto either incompletely noticed or not at all, would, when produced, appear capable of bearing the name of "discoveries"; with so little method and precision have the consequences of this fundamental axiom, "It is the greatest happiness of the greatest number that is the measure of right and wrong," been as yet developed. Be this as it may, if there be room for making and if there be use in publishing *discoveries* in the *natural* world, surely there is not much less room for making nor much less use in proposing *reformation* in the *moral.*

# Conclusion

There are two kinds of freedom. One is merely the absence of obstruction; it is essential; but it may be consistent with mere passivity. The second kind of freedom is strength or power, the ability to take action, or self-expression. It may be noted that there is in this second kind of freedom nothing which anyone would wish to restrict; on the contrary it is to the advantage of everyone to increase and use it.

Men have no freedom worth mentioning when they have no possibility of exercising their faculties and energy as they feel they must. Freedom in this dynamic sense cannot come to men, in all the abundance potential in our time, unless they collectively manage a large proportion of the social resources and economic equipment. The present economic waste by mismanagement is enormous; it is nothing but lost or unexploited strength; it constitutes a loss of freedom to many.

If the present economic system could unfailingly guarantee to rule out luck, force, fraud, misrepresentation, absentee ownership, the unmerited inheritance of wealth and therefore of irresponsible power; secure the equalization of educational opportunity and expunge unfair economic advantages; keep wide open the door to talent in every occupation; assure the dissolution of all monopolies; compel the pure, equal and instantaneous transmission of economic information to all producers and consumers, and make certain that scientific discoveries were immediately applied for the benefit of all, it would be a noble experiment to try private enterprise with relatively little governmental supplement for another fifty years — provided all started equal.

The inherent inability to make these changes is only too amply admitted by the managers of the present system in whispered candor among friends, and in not infrequent mutual recrimination. They are unable to solve three basic problems: (1) The system of competition by its very nature is a system of insecurity for all; and if unqualified in practice, it could stand for not more than a few days, after which there would be insufficient lampposts for its pedantic and trifling apologists. (2) There is a difference between the wealth of nations measured by the results of competition, and the wealth of nations measured by the values of a society of men and women who have lived together for centuries, and have, in the course of many social mutations and common vicissitudes, developed ideas of justice and human destiny, fairness, and reasonableness towards each other. These ideas cannot be segregated from the economic drives. (3) There are great economic works still which can be undertaken only by the state, whose parliamentarians and officers are so selected, and educated and motivated, and have such aptitudes, that they may add much to the wealth of the whole community, by their progressive ideas and enterprise.

If the maximum of freedom for all is to be available, then the maximum of economic welfare must be sought for all. This is not to confuse welfare and freedom. Economic welfare is a factor in freedom which requires property and income to allow men to realize their desires, and to substantiate the exercise of opportunity, faculties, and energies. There is a labyrinthine interfusion of welfare and freedom. These are not merely concrete things, that is pots and pans and the right to reside where one likes, but concepts that are significant in the degree we *feel* them to be. Where we freely reflect that a thing is wealth, it is wealth. When we freely reflect it is freedom, it is freedom. We may feel that less goods are desirable, if the result is to give us a greater feeling of freedom. Or we may feel that freedom is lacking, if the goods are not there to implement our own natural impulses, ideas, and faculties.

It is amazing what an enormous sphere of private freedom has been added to men by the increase of economic goods, especially in the leisure made available by shorter working hours and the inventions which make available to all the opportunities of pleasure, recreation, travel, the seven arts, reading, speculation, conversation, and electronic listening and seeing. And these add further to the capacity for untrammeled worship and the cultivation of family happiness.

There is no knowing exactly what fusion of welfare and freedom will suit the individual except by experience and trial. The pattern which will suit him will be found en route, not at the beginning of a long and unending adventure. Every economic system is a stage, not a fate. The world is still in the infant hours of civilization. The nineteenth century was not the beginning — nor the end, much as some economists may believe it to be. "The life of the law is not in logic, it is in experience." The future of individual good, then, is deeply involved in the whole long future of government. For it is in their own government that men can find the collective strength which will assure them of individual liberty. Popular self-government alone can marshal the power, that is the knowledge, the authority, and the ubiquity, to uphold the claims of all men to a satisfying admixture of wealth and freedom. It alone can solve the three problems above mentioned. The freedom of our time cannot possibly be an entire freedom from government, it can only be a freedom within government. The principal issue is to make sure that government is so constituted and conducted that it furnishes the prospect of advance according to the will of the majority and keeps the way back as well as the way forward continuously negotiable.

All men desire security as well as freedom. It is obvious that security guarantees freedom, for it is a safeguard against constraint by the irrational circumstances of the economy and by the managerial infirmities of economic individualists who are in possession of the productive machinery of society. Security is freedom to the extent that income offers the effective power to choose a way of action.

There is certainly no need to be terrified by the bogey that social security provision will petrify society into a condition of "status." For the social security of today and tomorrow may change whenever the millions are convinced that change is desirable. Modern social status, as distinct from that which prevailed in the murky dawn of civilization, is created by freedom of choice for all, in a society where rational action is assisted by the strong white light of science, and therefore soberly can be expected to be reasonable, temperate, modulated and evolving. All are, therefore, provided with a guarantee of freedom because all are provided with a guarantee of a portion in the power of self-government.

Three mighty developments of the last century and a half offer men a high degree both of welfare and of freedom. They are the great technological advances, already immense, and about to be even mightier servants of man, administrative science, and the principles and practice of democracy. It is for the latter two to use the first for humanity's advantage.

The intense focusing of attention on the rise of the competitive system and the division of labor during this period, and the enormous increase in the wealth of the world, have so dazzled the onlooker that the three factors we speak of have been overshadowed by the blaze. It is clear that before the modern division of labor there was an earlier form of it, and that the present one owes its victories not to itself, but to the fact that it was and is assisted by the rational use of advanced technology. Mechanical power and precision instruments of all kinds, not the division of labor, were the chief creators of contemporary wealth. These, however, no longer need to be managed and developed by an unlicensed set of economic enterprisers. Determination that invention should be developed and exploited in the service of man can best come from the community that is conscious of the pleasure obtainable from economic abundance. The community would not wish to frustrate invention as so many corporations do. This assumes that the administrative apparatus is available. It is. This is what the early nineteenth century lacked. But today we are conscious of its present uses, its difficult problems, and the solutions that the future demands. The apparatus is made in response to the desires of which it is the necessary instrument.

Above all, we have arrived at a technique and spirit of democratic government never equaled in human history, because there were never before such vast and dense agglomerations of human beings; never such a diffusion of knowledge and moral and practical wisdom; never such means of rapid communication among the people themselves and their myriad groupings. Immense areas have been reduced to the space-time-feeling dimensions of the single city of a hundred and fifty years ago.

Society as a whole, acting through its rationally constituted and deputed organs, is in a far better position than at any time in history to move forward to the collective management of many spheres of social life. When men attain to such a responsibility they certainly acquire freedom. This does not mean a government over all and everything. Society is now so able because what was before known only to individuals is now better known to social institutions, and can be even better known still through its own arrangements for the promotion and advancement of knowledge. Again, what was hitherto willed by individuals severally, and showed shortcomings in the consequent welfare for all, can be better willed and fulfilled by the social agents of all men freely choosing their purposes and deputies. The organs for fact-finding, analysis, interpretation, and the graduated and discriminating expression of popular approval and disapproval, were, in their contemporary quality, never before dreamed of. Finally, the organs of external control are sound and trustworthy.

Hence we have no reason to be afraid of our social strength, or the strength we care to lend to the government, or of the freedom we obtain as the result of using it through the organized medium — the social manager — which is government.

Since modern man is less bound, because he is technically more powerful and governmentally more aptly equipped, the question remains what does he will? His will demands abundance, justice, and freedom. These three are so involved in each other that the priority of one over the other cannot easily be discerned in general, though it can be in the battle for each separate law.

Abundance will be better obtained by far more confidence in the management by social administration of sectors of the national economy. The competitive system is irredeemably caught in the dark, tangled wood of its own egoisms, hostilities, frictions, and rigidities, the inevitable product of its own premises — egoism, and therefore severity; insecurity, and therefore fear and therefore offensive and defensive measures for its own security. Power, not being socially responsible, is abused in such a system, and limits the production of goods for private advantage.

Justice is the great unknown quantity of political philosophy. Pascal said that man is ignorant of it. Yet man must act as though he were not. Justice is not a self-contained con-

226

stant capsule, or a gift, or an instinct, with sure, objective, and unchanging contours. It is a relationship between men in society; and, revealed to individual minds in the passage of time, it is accepted in the shape and degree which are tolerable to all at the speed at which all can tolerate change. This process can surely never be better midwived than by popular sovereignty and the process of discovery by free debate. If it were not to risk the mixture of like and unlike, we could recommend Justice Holmes's opinion that the best test of truth (say, justice) "is the power of the thought to get itself accepted in the competition of the market. . . . It is an experiment, as all life is an experiment." Justice is recognized, revealed, stimulated by the play of competitors in the broad and open forum of politics. Justice in our time is above all likely to mean an appropriate degree of economic welfare and a settled insistence on the career open to the talents.

The regulator and producer of abundance and justice is public freedom, and this also creates those private felicities and security which constitute private freedom, in the sense of the capacity for continuous initiative. Public freedom unreservedly demands free association, election and recall of government, freedom of speech, writing, opinion, and opposition. It is within these that men learn their responsibility that marches with their endowment of authority, the common sense and tact of more than everyday affairs. The prospects of its free and advantageous use have been immensely improved by the remarkably able and at the same time magnanimous use of the power of democratic society in the successful conduct of World War II. Free government has truly come of age, and offers, to the millions upon millions whose minds and characters have never yet been given the opportunity to contribute to the common good, a broad avenue of advancement. Men have the right to comprehend and employ their confidence, and to make of their increas-

227

ing abundance and power a yet more sensitive justice and
more abundant freedom. With Walt Whitman, social democracy may respond, to the bare, poor, deprecating, and
unsuccessful philosophy of "Snatch!" which is the spirit of
economic individualism: —

> Come, I will make the continent indissoluble,
> I will make the most splendid race the sun ever shone
> upon.